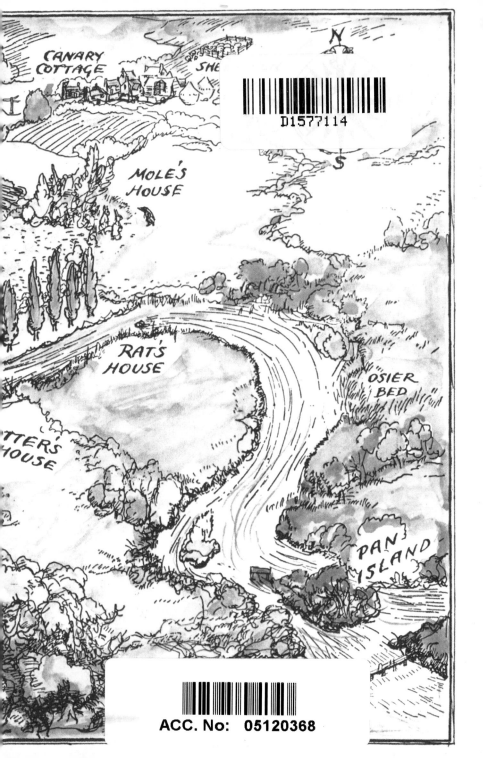

Eternal Boy

MATTHEW DENNISON is the author
of seven critically acclaimed works of
non-fiction, and a contributor to
Country Life and the *Telegraph*.

Eternal Boy

The Life of
Kenneth Grahame

MATTHEW DENNISON

An Apollo Book

For my father, who loves *The Wind in the Willows*
and boats and the sea

And
a River went out of
Eden.

'What the Boy chiefly dabbled in was natural history and fairy-tales, and he just took them as they came, in a sandwichy sort of way, without making any distinctions; and really his course of reading strikes one as rather sensible.'

Kenneth Grahame, 'The Reluctant Dragon'

Contents

· 1 ·

'Brown sails, blue water and Highlanders'

I F WE IMAGINE Kenneth Grahame as a child as he described himself, he is doodling in the margins of a book. It is 1866 or thereabouts and he is seven years old.

He draws crocodiles of jagged outline and spear-bearing African tribesmen, licking the lead of his pencil to make each mark decisively black. He draws monkeys 'gibbering with terror', swarming up palm trees, and admits that an oak tree is beyond his skills. Most of the books he decorates are histories of the ancient world. He singles out Macaulay's *Lays of Ancient Rome*, a Victorian schoolroom staple. Afterwards his doodles are imprinted on his mind more vividly than Hannibal's stirring triumphs or 'the ornate set speeches' of Roman generals, whose voices – 'powerless to pierce the distance' of time – echo thin and faint. His pencil prefers exotica. In place of centurions or legionary banners he draws 'the more attractive flesh and blood of animal life, the varied phases of tropic forest'. He 'note[s], cite[s], and illustrate[s] the habits of crocodiles'.[1] On the flyleaf he draws 'ships and battles'.[2]

Like his pencil, his mind wanders with a boy's unruly imagination. He amuses himself playing games with words. 'By this single battle of Magnesia, Antiochus the Great lost all his conquests in Asia,' he reads, and he substitutes 'bottle' for 'battle'. Some margins he leaves blank. 'The white spaces are "clear sky" ever through which

I could sail away at will to more gracious worlds' in the words of his river- and boat-loving adult self.[3] He calls his 'gracious worlds' 'cloudland', the descriptor already coined by Robert Louis Stevenson. Sometimes he labels it 'Elfland' or 'Poppyland', suggesting by turns fairy tales, which he loves, or oblivion. All his daydreams are escapist – of crocodiles or tribesmen or monkeys – though he is lying on the nursery floor or in the drawing room, 'in my sub-world of chair legs and hearth-rugs and the undersides of sofas'.[4]

At the same time the young Kenneth comes across an old-fashioned atlas. Its maps include empty passages where the mapmaker's knowledge has run out. Later he described these voids lingeringly, remembering the excitement of first encounter: 'broad buff spaces... unbroken by the blue of any lake, crawled upon by no mountain ranges'.[5] Like the margins round Macaulay's verse, the blanks inspire his drawing, as well as daydreams of 'a dozen clamorous cities of magic, and... room for a prairie or two, a Sahara, and a brand new set of Rockies'. Best of all, his mind's eye glimpses 'kingdoms yet to discover, and golden realms that await their Marco Polo... shimmering with barbaric pearl and gold'.[6] He takes out his paint box. 'The obstinate lid... jams and slides a little, and jams again... the crimson lake sticks to the Prussian blue, and the gamboge persists in "rucking up" when the lid has to be pushed back.'[7]

Dark-haired, pale-faced and short for his age, Kenneth Grahame was an imaginative child; he became an imaginative adult. He continued to invent 'golden realms' into old age; he let his thoughts take wing, and the playfulness of those thoughts remained boyish. 'As the highest expression of the emotion of Joy, we would all of us naturally choose to spring upon a charger and ride forth into the boundless prairie,' he wrote in 1925, at the age of sixty-six.[8] He likened personal fantasy to a 'fourth dimension' or parallel universe: 'side by side with the other life... always there, always handy to step into', a 'crowded and coloured panorama' that his inner eye saw clearly.[9] He celebrated its richly visual qualities and insisted on its reality. By comparison he dismissed as inanities, delusions and 'pale phantasms' adult preoccupations like politics and society, childlike in his contempt for the mundane.[10] 'Real life', asserts the boy-narrator of one of a series of celebrated stories he wrote in his thirties, lies outside the drawing room and the scope of grown-up convention. In the orchard, the fir wood, the hazel copse and the duck pond are to be found magic and portents and robbers' caves and hidden treasure, the 'real' ingredients of Kenneth's own childhood games. He insisted that 'a dragon... is a more enduring animal than a pterodactyl... every honest person believes in dragons – down in the back-kitchen of his consciousness': his own belief was unshakeable.[11] Revealing aspects of his doodling, dreaming younger self, he insisted on the hermetic, *excluding* nature of a child's imagination and the solitariness of his own child-like fantasies. Pitilessly he described a mother in church. With delight she notes 'the rapt, absorbed air of her little son, during the course of a sermon that is stirring her own very vitals': 'Ten to one he is a thousand miles away, safe in his own kingdom; and what is more, he has shut the door behind him. *She* is left outside, with the parson and the clerk.'[12]

Imaginative escape moulded Kenneth Grahame's child-hood. It found expression in the scribbled margins of books and swashbuckling games played out in his head under the influence of Ballantyne's *The Dog Crusoe and His Master*, a story of prairie settlers, *Aesop's Fables* or newly published descriptions of the Nile by explorer Samuel Baker. Afterwards it dominated his memories. It provided threads of narrative that he pursued in his writing as well as his interior life, and the excitement of childish adventure and childhood stories never palled for him. He was a quiet child. When, seldom, he sat for a photographer, he appeared earnest or bored, and nothing of his heroic self-fashioning showed in his startled, blank gawping so typical of early photographs, with their long exposures and enforced stillness. Hard to trace in that unrevealing gaze traces of 'the small boy [thrust] out under the naked heavens to enact a sorry and shivering Crusoe on an islet in the duck-pond' or so consumed by excitement at the prospect of a circus that he longs 'to escape into the open air, to shake off bricks and mortar, and to wander in the unfrequented places of the earth, the more properly to take in the passion and the promise of this giddy situation'.[13]

In an essay called 'Long Odds', he recalled his six- or seven-year-old self. He depicted a boy of fluid identity, able to shape-shift at will. The boy is so absorbed in fantasy that he *becomes* his fictional hero. 'In the person of his hero of the hour [he] can take on a Genie... a few Sultans and a couple of hostile armies, with a calmness resembling indifference.'[14] He has 'a healthy appetite for pirates, a neat hand at the tomahawk, and a simple passion for being marooned'. If, like Ballantyne's hero, he 'sall[ies] out to deal with a horde of painted Indians', the only defence he needs is 'his virtue and his unerring smoothbore'.[15] The ten-year-old hero of his story 'A Saga of the Seas' captains a bathtub in the centre of the nursery floor. He triumphs over icebergs, polar bears, pirates and picaroons, rocking the tub on an overturned towel horse. Singlehandedly he sees off the full-grown pirate chief, 'a fine, black-bearded fellow in his way, but hardly up to date in his parry-and-thrust business'.[16] Neither boy acknowledges obstacles or deterrents. They are rewarded with 'ingots and Mexican dollars and church plate... ropes of pearls... and big stacks of nougat; and rubies and gold watches and Turkish Delight in tubs', a delightfully jumbled account of the late-Victorian wish list, in which imperial greed contends with a child's sweet tooth.[17] Both boys' stories include fragments of self-portrait: Kenneth Grahame was that boy at six and at ten – and, in imagination, ever after.

As a child in 'cloudland' he circled the globe – like Puck, or like the part-fictionalized boys of his stories, or in his other guise of crocodile-doodling reader. He always came home. Ideas of escape and homecoming, twinned from childhood, mark the pendulum swing of his mind. They shape his only full-length fiction, *The Wind in the Willows*. Doggedly he embraced his own parallel universe as a reality and sugared it with guarantees of a safe return. In a similar way, in *The Odyssey*, a poem Kenneth Grahame knew well and plundered in *The Wind in the Willows*, Homer tempers the reader's experience of Odysseus's terrifying exploits with assurances of his fated homecoming. The certainty of a safe return as a corollary to escape, 'the world shut out... the ideal encasement', as Kenneth described it, was one source of happiness in his fragmented, peripatetic, orphaned and exiled childhood.[18]

And childhood happiness is not least among the surprises of his life.

He began well enough, with what he afterwards labelled 'a proper equipment of parents'.[19]

Kenneth Grahame was born on 8 March 1859, in Edinburgh. 32 Castle Street was, as it remains, foursquare and handsome. Generous in its proportions, restrainedly neoclassical, it is typical of domestic architecture in Edinburgh's New Town. Shallow steps rise to a front door topped by an elegant but simple fanlight. Glazing bars neatly bisect tall windows. The house is built of granite the colour of watercolour shadows. Kenneth's first biographer places an almond tree outside it. Its branches stretch tight-furled buds towards first-floor windows.[20] The same author, harried by Kenneth's fanciful widow, furnishes those branches retrospectively with a single bird, a thrush from nearby Princes Street Gardens. Inevitably it heralds the new arrival in song.

In truth, it was a morning of brittle cold, with few intimations of spring. Scuds of snow lingered in the gutters, the wind as sharp and glancing as a knife blade. Inside, chloroform eased the pangs of the twenty-two-year-old mother, pretty Bessie Grahame. Dr James Simpson, who attended her, had made his name over the last decade as a pioneer of the miraculous, controversial and still highly dangerous anaesthetic: a short, whiskery man of humble background and cosy appearance and professor of mid-wifery at Edinburgh's university. He did not remain long enough after delivery to weigh the newborn baby; his estimate of eight pounds was an accurate one. While Bessie rested after her ordeal, her baby slept in his crib beside her bed. Afterwards he was removed to the nursery and the company of Ferguson the nurse and his older siblings – Helen, then three, and year-old Thomas William, called Willie. Five years would pass before a third son, Roland, completed the close-knit family.

Before that, Kenneth's birth was another milestone in the happy marriage of James Cunningham Grahame and Bessie Inglis. Lawyer and merchant's daughter, they enjoyed social position and a degree of material comfort. On the female side, the Grahames traced a double line of descent from Robert the Bruce. At a distance, Scottish nobles peppered the family tree. More recently, Grahame men had served as accountants or, like Kenneth's father, lawyers. *Defence of Usury Laws* of 1817, *Financial Fenianism and the Caledonian Railway* of 1867 and *Tables of Silver Exchanges* of 1890, written by successive James Grahames, suggest aptitude in their particular spheres, if something short of literary fireworks, and a sterling commitment to respectability. Over the literary exploits of an earlier James Grahame, the family drew a veil. Abandoning the Scottish bar for an Anglican curacy, in 1809 he had published a lengthy devotional poem, *The Sabbath*, punctuated by the joyless refrain, 'Hail, Sabbath! thee I hail, the poor man's day.' This dog-in-the-manger versifying earned him Byron's dismissal in *English Bards and Scotch Reviewers* as 'Sepulchral Grahame'. Instead of springing to his defence, his descendants preferred to ignore him. Like the shepherd in Kenneth's story 'The Reluctant Dragon', they '[didn't] hold with art and poetry much'.[21] The instinct for respectability had its repressive side.

Inheritance is frequently unreliable. Evidently Kenneth's father lacked the Calvinist convictions of so many of his forebears, dark prognostications about earthly pleasure. A romantic, poetry-loving streak linked him to Sepulchral Grahame, a strain of melancholy. His particular weakness was not poetry or morbid Anglicanism but claret: domestic felicity failed to bring about a cure. Following the births of his children, his alcoholic cravings grew. As a young man he had made a splash in his chosen career. His advocacy had a witty tang. He was quoted by his peers, admired, earmarked for success. In the face of escalating dependency his professional judgement faltered.

Whether it was Cunningham Grahame himself – bookish, pessimistic and prey to black moods – or practical, dauntless Bessie who evolved a scheme to preserve the family from shameful exposure is not recorded. Baby Kenneth would spend little more than a year in the house in Castle Street. In May 1860, the Grahames left the capital, never to return. Afterwards Kenneth remembered nothing of Edinburgh's dignified thoroughfares, the ancient fortress on its mound, even his father's tales of the house nearby, once home to Walter Scott. In appearance, 32 Castle Street suggests gentle sensibilities and financial certainties. Appearances are misleading. Cunningham Grahame's drinking jeopardized both and neither would play much part in Kenneth's childhood.

The Grahames took flight to Ardrishaig, on the tree-studded western slopes of Loch Fyne close to the mouth of the Crinan Canal, where Gaelic-speaking locals eked out a living fishing the loch waters for herring or busy about the harbour, a place 'of brown sails, blue water and Highlanders'.[22] From Edinburgh the family travelled first by train. Kenneth claimed the occasion afterwards as the source of his earliest memory, of 'shiny black buttons, buttons that dug into dusty, blue cloth': the railway carriage upholstery.[23] By paddle steamer they completed their journey over the loch's deep, inky waters, past green rises shadowed by clouds. Despite the opening of the canal half a century earlier and its traffic in passenger steamers made fashionable by Queen Victoria's visit in 1847, Ardrishaig was an out-of-the-way place. 'The steadfast mystery of [its] horizon', Kenneth's later measure of unspoiled landscape, had not yet been obliterated by railway lines or new building.[24] For Cunningham and Bessie Grahame, its single main street and small spider's web smattering of modest houses were a far cry from the squares and terraces of the New Town. In an image he used in *The Wind in the Willows* to describe the feelings of Portly the otter cub when he is discovered by Ratty and Mole, Kenneth recalled his own response to this first uprooting: 'as a child that has fallen happily asleep in its nurse's arms, and wakes to find itself... laid in a strange place'.[25]

Annfield Lodge, Ardrishaig, in which were shortly installed parents, children, household and nursery staff and, in time, a pair of Cairn terriers from the Isle of Jura, was all but new. With bay windows and pointed gables and surrounded by large gardens, it overlooked the loch. Given its distance from Inveraray, some thirty miles to the north, where Cunningham Grahame's work required him frequently, it was scarcely a practical choice, and the Grahames were to move again to a house in nearby Lochgilphead before finally settling full time in Inveraray itself. Until then they took a lease on two houses, although a local official dismissed the small Inveraray house where Cunningham spent his working weeks without his wife and children as 'quite unsuitable for a family residence'.[26] His separation from Bessie for much of this period accounts for the lengthy interval between her third and fourth pregnancies.

The Grahames' westerly migration was the result of a new job for Cunningham. In the late spring of 1860, he was appointed sheriff-substitute for Argyll – a judge with responsibility for the county's civil and criminal courts. In worldly terms, it was almost certainly a demotion for a man so recently among the rising stars of Edinburgh's Parliament House. Inveraray's remoteness, the more meagre distractions of the west coast and escape from the Grahames' busy social life offered hope that Cunningham would avoid further downward spiralling, and in the short term this may indeed have been the case. He seems to have set about his new duties without regret for the legal life of the capital.

Yet his state of mind was ambivalent. Kenneth remembered walks with his father along the loch shore. On good days Cunningham beguiled the minutes in storytelling, the children entranced, like Kenneth's description in *The Wind in the Willows* of Mole's first experience of the river, the bewitched Mole trotting along the banks 'as one trots, when very small, by the side of a man who holds one spellbound by exciting stories'.[27] At other times his father recited Longfellow.

To Helen, Willie and Kenneth, Cunningham's choice must have seemed appropriate:

> I remember the black wharves and the slips,
> And the sea-tides tossing free;
> And Spanish sailors with bearded lips
> And the beauty and mystery of the ships,
> And the magic of the sea.

They did not know the poem's title, 'My Lost Youth'. Nor could a very young child, as Kenneth was, absorb the verses' full poignancy or identify what it was that drew Cunningham to them – self-absorption, unhappiness or, possibly, straightforward poetic enjoyment. The poem's refrain would become for Kenneth a mission statement: 'A boy's will is the wind's will,/ And the thoughts of youth are long, long thoughts.' Like the poem's narrator, for the rest of his life daydreaming Kenneth would conjure from air 'islands that were the Hesperides/ Of all my boyish dreams.'

Cunningham Grahame's new posting brought the family within the orbit of George Campbell, 8th duke of

Argyll. The shadow of the duke's iron-grey Gothick castle hovered over Inveraray. At the end of the previous century his grandfather had rebuilt the small town. In the wake of Cunningham's appointment, the duke offered him land on which to build a house, which Cunningham declined. The duke's response, considered by locals surprisingly liberal, was an agreement early in 1862 that he himself would 'build a large and handsome house for the Sheriff'.[28]

It was completed the following year: a substantial granite building, the work of the duke's architect George Devey. In the early stages of her fourth pregnancy, Bessie Grahame oversaw its furnishing; in the garden she planted cuttings of roses and white broom sent from her parents' house at Lasswade in Midlothian. Only the roses flourished. Three years had passed since the Grahames' departure from Edinburgh. For Kenneth, who was too young to remember that earlier life, there had been delights in the family's lochside nomadism. The tang of sea kelp that spiked the salt air along the loch shore; a model wooden boat, *The Canty Queen*, given to him by its maker, Rory McGilp the fisherman; outdoor games with Bhodach and Cailliach the terriers, and a large black dog of unidentified breed called Don; sticky gingerbread sold in the children's favourite of Ardrishaig's shops; the cockatoo belonging to a Mrs Jenkins that shrieked from its cage at passers-by; nests of water voles, which Kenneth called 'water rats', along the banks of the Crinan Canal; 'a splash of white foam over the brim/ Of a dusty pool... / A flood of ripples and sunlit spray'[29]; and 'the ever recurrent throb of [the steamer's] paddle-wheel, the rush and foam of beaten water among the piles, splash of ropes and rumble of gangways, and all the attendant hurry and scurry' of the pierside.[30] Only some continued in Inveraray.

In Inveraray, nursery life followed routines established by Ferguson in Castle Street and Ardrishaig. From the nursery windows, Helen, Willie and Kenneth gazed out over broad expanses of the loch, busy with boats and birds, the sounds of the water ever present. The garden was big enough for adventure, for secret places and solitariness. And downstairs, Cunningham and Bessie's lives resumed something of their former buoyant roundelay. In the autumn, they were invited to dine at Inveraray Castle with the duke and duchess and the duke's unmarried sister, Lady Emma. Bessie beguiled the duchess with her easy vivacity and good looks that corresponded nearly enough to contemporary ideals: dark hair, a limpid gaze, rosebud lips. The duke's heir, Lord Lorne, expressed delight at meeting the twin sister of his Eton rowing hero, David Inglis. The following day, by invitation, Bessie returned to the Castle with Helen. Neither Helen nor the duke's daughters appear to have taken pains to forge anything resembling friendly acquaintance. The duchess loaned Bessie one of the Castle's gardeners – too late for the cuttings of white broom, which had died already.

This ducal imprimatur marked the beginning of a new life for the Grahames. It proved of short duration. On 16 March 1864, Bessie gave birth to her third son. Within days, she had succumbed to scarlet fever. For a fortnight her life hung in the balance. She died on 4 April at the age of twenty-seven, and her last words, no more than a whisper, were the simple but affecting, 'It's all been so lovely.'

· 2 ·

'Happy, heedless victims'

'I LIKE BEST the wanderings of little George and his indomitable father on the open road with its ale-houses and toll-gates, over commons or on wayside strips of grass,' wrote a wistful Kenneth Grahame late in life, in a preface he contributed to the life of circus impresario George Sanger.[1] He last walked with his own father when he was five years old, listening to Longfellow on the banks of Loch Fyne.

For some time Kenneth knew nothing of his mother's death; he too fell victim to scarlet fever. Like Bessie, he oscillated for days between collapse and recovery. Cunningham's mother sat at his bedside, summoned from Edinburgh, and distracted him with memories of her girlhood: the long, slow journey half a century earlier of the Edinburgh mail coach to London; the thrill of opening for the first time the latest novel by Walter Scott.

'Why does a coming bereavement project no thin faint voice, no shadow of its woe to warn its happy, heedless victims?' Kenneth wrote in 1898 in a story called 'A Departure'.[2] In 1864 he was too young for such thoughts. He had lost two parents at once. The death of his mother was the easier to comprehend. In its wake, despair, unhappiness and an unalterable self-pity overwhelmed his brooding father: so, too, an alcoholic torpor he was powerless to shrug off.

Cunningham collapsed into angry befuddlement. As in 1860, the Grahames acted quickly. A family conference decided to remove Helen, Willie, Kenneth and baby Roland from their father's doubtful care. They were sent to England with Ferguson the nurse, to their maternal grandmother and another new beginning on the green banks of the Thames – in Kenneth's case, taking with him his kilt and a rubber ball bought en route in a toyshop in Stirling, the temporary comforter of this lost little child. Perhaps the station porter noticed his misery. Long afterwards he described a 'good-natured' railwayman, who tells a rhyme to a child boarding a train: 'This is the tree that never grew, this is the bird that never flew; this is the fish that never swam, this is the bell that never rang.'[3] The only evidence that Cunningham, punch-drunk with grief, resisted family diaspora is his request two years later that his motherless children return to him.

For Kenneth and his siblings there were to be no more untroubled mornings of low mist across the loch, the swoop of gulls, the echoing percussion of boats at anchor or the thrum of steamers. No more would they hear soft Gaelic music in fishermen's mouths, the coarse ribaldry of the fisher girls who threaded lug worms for bait onto hooks or emptied the cold, shining, stinking catch into baskets. For Kenneth the backdrop of cloud-shrugged hills would recede into a dim past, those shadowy slopes spotted with sturdy trees. Bar a single disastrous return to his father's house in Inveraray and subsequent sojourns on the Continent, for the remainder of his life Kenneth Grahame lived in England – a life of mostly conventional middle-class Englishness. 'The gleaming lochs and sinuous firths of the Western Highlands, where, twice a week maybe, [a train] crept by headland and bay,' were consigned to memory – or imagining.[4]

Unconsulted, Helen, Willie, Kenneth and Roland acquired a new home. It lay in the Berkshire village of Cookham Dean, at the furthest reach of old Windsor Forest – as Kenneth described it, 'King Alfred's country, probably much as it was 1,000 years ago', a 'sequestered reach of the quiet Thames'.[5] Surrounded by 'crowding laurels', copper beeches and 'high-standing elms', The Mount had grown with the centuries, a higgledy-piggledy house with leaded windows and half-timbering and its roof of clay tiles well weathered. Outside there were lily ponds, an orchard, rows of raspberry canes, meadow grass thick with buttercups.[6] The garden was terraced over several levels. Beyond unfurled a broad ribbon of river, slowed by weirs and overhung by willow trees and alders – quite different from the sea-like expanse of Loch Fyne – and dense, dark, thickly carpeted Quarry Wood. How any of the children felt on arrival is matter for conjecture. Kenneth referred once to the child's 'readiness to welcome a perfect miracle at any hour of the day or night'.[7]

The guardian chosen for the young Grahames was Bessie's mother, Mary Inglis, a sternly competent widow of sixty encased in black silk moiré, autocratic in temperament, with the same hooded eyes and long, straight nose she had bequeathed her daughter; only the lines of her mouth had settled into a dour grimace. The youngest of her five sons, Bessie's rowing twin David, newly appointed to the curacy of Cookham Dean, lived with her. His modest stipend failed to relieve her persistent anxiety about money.

By family decree it was Cunningham's brother John, another widower, who took financial responsibility for his nephews and niece. Like Mrs Inglis, John Grahame had left his native Scotland for the south of England and employment as a parliamentary agent; he became a partner in the firm of Grahame, Currie and Spens. In their different ways grandmother and uncle imbued the Grahames' childhood with distinctively Scots values. Mrs Inglis's Presbyterianism was of an unassertive variety; her kindness, Kenneth claimed, extended no further than 'the needs of the flesh' and he mistrusted lifelong 'the shadow of Scotch-Calvinist devil-worship'.[8] 'I don't suppose she could be described as a child lover,' was Helen's terse verdict.[9] She was predictably strict over table manners. Her storytelling included folklore and Scottish ballads; the children surely missed their mother's levity, her laughter like 'an irreverent angel'.[10] Instead, kindness was the province of David Inglis. He introduced the children to the river and, as Helen remembered, 'made a great deal of us'; to Mrs Inglis's matriarchal fiefdom he introduced the vicar of Cookham Dean, George Hewitt Hodson, a classicist and editor of a volume of letters from India – like the rector in Kenneth's story 'A Harvesting', who 'was alleged to have written a real book'.[11] For his part, Uncle John Grahame took pains that liberality never overmastered prudence. With some bitterness Kenneth would identify indifference as the keynote of this stand-in parenting. He attributed it to stupidity.

He responded by withdrawing into imaginary relationships and imaginary worlds. 'Whenever a child is set down in a situation that is distasteful, out of harmony, jarring,' his adult self theorized, 'that very moment he begins without conscious effort to throw out and to build up an environment really suitable to his soul, and to transport himself thereto.'[12] 'Dreams are but re-action from life,' he told an audience in 1921, 'and the easiest, the most accessible form of healing re-action that there is.'[13] As a result the influence on him of grandmother and uncles was less than that of The Mount itself. In his stubborn, floundering loneliness, the uneven old house, with its heavy wooden beams and broad hearths and gardens close to the river, exercised a kind of enchantment. Best of all was the attic. The children christened it the 'Gallery': large enough for games, distant from Mrs Inglis, a holiday world of misrule and topsy-turvydom.

For the remainder of his life, The Mount set the perimeters for Kenneth's dreaming. In the stories he published to considerable acclaim in *The Golden Age* and *Dream Days*, the memories he plundered are of this childhood home: the garden, the 'Gallery', the neighbouring village, fields and the river, their reality greater than the grief he never mentioned. These stories – for adults – relate episodes in the life of a family of five children: Edward, Selina, Charlotte, Harold and a narrator who is not named. The children have neither mother nor father, but inhabit a parentless house, in which authority is exercised by a repeatedly worsted camarilla of aunts and visiting uncles – mostly regarded by the narrator with disdain – and a governess who inspires more complex emotions. The children devote their leisure hours to vigorous play-acting or dreamy escapism. On his own, the narrator communes with nature 'by instinct', hearing 'the grass-blades thrust and sprout', or kneels on the hearthrug, 'soft and wide, with the thickest of pile', flicking greedily through picture books that thrill him 'with a vision of blues and reds... pictures all highly coloured' or, alternatively, images of 'a tiger seized by a crocodile while drinking'.[14] The adult Kenneth acknowledged an autobiographical aspect to these 'fictions'.[15] It was at The Mount that he became a doodler and a dreamer. There his fancy was ignited by the natural world of the garden and, beyond it, Quarry Wood and the Thames: there, like Rat in *The Wind in the Willows*, he became, as he would remain, 'a self-sufficing sort of animal, rooted to the land'. At The Mount he learned that 'if you lay down your nose an inch or two from the water, it was not long ere the old sense of proportion vanished clean away. The glittering insects that darted to and fro on its surface became sea-monsters dire, the gnats that hung above them swelled to albatrosses, and the pond itself stretched out into a vast inland sea'.[16] At The Mount he dreamed, like 'most other boys of my own age and period, the mighty mid-Victorian', of longed-for presents, aligning his rootless orphaned childhood hankerings with those of his contemporaries. One dream recurred. 'On some wonderful morning one would be awakened by the sound of a pawing and crunching of the gravel outside... one would spring from bed with beating heart, would fling wide the lattice-window and looking down would see on the carriage-drive a neatly attired groom holding the bridle of a peerless pony, a cream-coloured pony – it was always cream-coloured – with a long flowing tail (it always had a long flowing tail).'[17] Of course that morning never came.

Mrs Inglis was not at pains to staunch her grandchildren's grief. Ferguson's presence and a household of female servants notwithstanding, she was an old woman to take on the care of three small children and a baby. Her precarious financial position troubled her. With rigid logic John Grahame repeatedly urged upon her the soundness of leaving The Mount for somewhere smaller and more manageable. She had exerted herself in pulling strings wherever possible on her sons' behalf: by the time of Bessie's death, her energies were depleted. *The Golden Age* and *Dream Days* suggest that the children were cast on their own resources. In Kenneth's case he burrowed ever deeper into that make-believe world more real and more compelling to him than the incomprehensible misery of parental loss and lovelessness, from which he never recovered: mentally he turned his back on a 'life... so rough to him, so full of pricks and jogs, and smartings'.[18] This solution was his own. Brisk, unimaginative Helen and gentler Willie, whose health was poor, were equally unhappy. All three were too young to help one another. 'In moments of mental depression, nothing is quite so consoling as the honest smell of a painted animal,' Kenneth offered later, recalling his attachment in childhood to his toys, a statement of bleak isolation.[19] At first he had the rubber ball from the toyshop in Stirling. The kilt was quickly outgrown.

The rudderless trauma underlying Kenneth's childhood addiction to fantasy inspired his love of circuses and country fairs, with their invitation 'in imagination to swim in golden lagoons and wander through parrot-haunted jungles.'[20] Realms of spectacle and sensation, the circus and the fair offered excitement and dramatic escape; both possessed the power to make him dizzy with happiness throughout his life. Emotions were mostly excluded from his adventure games, displaced by action, 'excitement and mystery, curiosity and suspense.'[21] The appeal of the circus was a superficial thing, plumbing no more depths than a pancake.

And Kenneth's springboard into happy unreality was consistently The Mount. Lacking mother or father, his sibling fellowship only partly congenial, at The Mount this thoughtful orphan did achieve a measure of febrile happiness. The golden interlude lasted two years. Until his death Kenneth remembered it, and his reactions to it, with absolute clarity. 'I feel I should never be surprised to meet myself as I was when a little chap of five, suddenly coming round a corner,' he speculated in 1907. 'I can remember everything I felt then, the part of my brain I used from four till about seven can never have altered... After that time I don't remember anything particularly.'[22]

The years of intensest feeling were those in his grandmother's house in Cookham Dean, although Mrs Inglis herself impacts not at all on future reminiscence. His experiences at The Mount fixed a habit of engaging with places above people. Ever after, Kenneth's recorded memories are dominated by descriptions of setting: landscape, townscape, buildings, nature. He approached the world from a position of self-containment, as a watchful observer, albeit not always a detached observer – like the protagonist in Robert Louis Stevenson's essay 'An Apology for Idlers', which he read later: 'As a matter of fact, an intelligent person, looking out of his eyes and hearkening in his ears, with a smile on his face all the time, will get more true education than many another in a life of heroic vigils.'[23] In Kenneth's case the smile came and went, for there would be no return to The Mount.

Collapsing masonry brought about expulsion from his Thames-side Eden. Heavy winds in December 1865 felled one of The Mount's chimneystacks. It was the excuse Uncle John Grahame needed to convince Mrs Inglis that moving was imperative.

With a heavy heart, Mary Inglis concurred. The Mount was sold and she accepted the offer of a lease on Fern Hill Cottage, Cranbourne, a dozen miles southeast of Cookham Dean. The move took place the following spring, around the time of Kenneth's birthday. With neither The Mount's large garden nor the 'Gallery' attic, and beyond easy reach of the river, Fern Hill Cottage became seven-year-old Kenneth's sixth home. What he thought about it can only be inferred from his silence, since no mention of it survives in his published work or his letters. The move coincided with the point – identified later – at which his memory ceased.

There were further upheavals in store. Cunningham Grahame wrote to request the return of his children from his mother-in-law. Again Mrs Inglis concurred. The children made the long journey by train, accompanied by Ferguson, 'through the furnace-lit Midlands, and on till the grey glimmer of dawn showed stone walls in place of hedges... till the bright sun shone upon brown leaping streams and purple heather, and the clear, sharp northern air streamed in through the windows', and so back, once more, to the big new granite house in Inveraray where their mother – and a portion of their childhood – had died.[24]

Whatever Cunningham Grahame's wishes, his resolve proved inadequate to the task of parenting singlehandedly.

Over the course of 1866, his good intentions fell victim to his drinking. He could not manage the four young children so desperately in need of parental reassurance. He could no longer manage the responsibilities of the position of sheriff substitute. He gave up both, with little choice in either decision. Through his resignation he forfeited the house overlooking the loch. He did not look for another, but left Inveraray for France and an unlovely boarding house in Le Havre, where Grahame, Currie and Spens had an outpost, and twenty twilight years tutoring for small beer. He left behind Helen, Willie, Kenneth and Roland and made no attempt to contact them again.

The children returned to Mrs Inglis and the confines of Fern Hill Cottage. David Inglis's absence, following his marriage in 1866, added to the bleakness of their 'home'-coming. However limited their understanding, the three older children had all witnessed something of their father's ignominy, though none ever spoke of it. In secret Helen began to write poetry. Kenneth's response made its way into print three decades later. 'Grown-up people really ought to be more careful. Among themselves it may seem but a small thing to give their word and take back their word... But with those who are below them, whose little globe is swayed by them, who rush to build star-pointing alhambras on their most casual word, they really ought to be more careful.'[25]

Among the figures that dominate Kenneth's non-fiction essays, published after Cunningham's death, is the man who runs away – an enduring source of fascination. Surprisingly the author treats him leniently. In the stories of Edward, Selina, Charlotte, Harold and the unnamed narrator, he grants fewer concessions. In these stories adults are 'hopeless and incapable', commanding no respect, blind 'to anything but appearances': a 'strange anaemic order of beings' further removed from children 'than the kindly beasts who shared our natural existence in the sun'.[26] They are 'the Olympians', an honorific bitter in its irony. None of the five children laments a father's absence. More unexpectedly, the stories contain no idealization of a mother's role, and their substitute mothers – obtuse, unthinking Aunt Eliza and Miss Smedley the governess – scarcely impact upon their charges; Aunt Eliza is an object of exasperation or contempt. In spirit, Kenneth's fictional children are autonomous and independent, as orphans must become. But they are not invulnerable. They are 'entirely at [the Olympians'] mercy... their butt, their martyr, their drudge'.[27] When it occurs, unhappiness is strong enough to last a lifetime. 'The crude blank misery of a moment,' Kenneth wrote in 1895, 'is apt to leave a dull bruise which is slow to depart, if it ever do so entirely.'[28]

· 3 ·

'Rubs and knocks
and competition'

'THIS STRANGE UNKNOWN thing called school,' Kenneth wrote, in a story in which the eldest of his five fictional children, Edward, departs, bowler-hatted, by train for life outside the nursery, 'had always been before us as an inevitable bourne.'[1] Neither Willie nor Kenneth can have doubted its inevitability. Boys' boarding school was a rite of passage for the Victorian middle classes, as it would remain. And Fern Hill Cottage was smaller than The Mount to accommodate Mrs Inglis and her servants and four growing children and their nurse.

The new St Edward's School in Oxford, which opened in 1863, recommended itself to sensible Uncle John Grahame on account of its cheapness. Fees were set at £25 a year, 'within the reach of parents of moderate means', as its founder intended.[2] In place of the gentlemanly leisure targeted by better-known schools, it prepared its leavers for employment. Kenneth arrived in the autumn of 1868, aged nine and a half.

To date his education had consisted of the usual home schooling in the nursery, delivered by whichever forgotten preceptor also taught Helen and Willie. Latin lessons with a local clergyman supplemented the nursery grounding in maths, reading and the more colourful aspects of the humanities – what Kenneth dismissed as 'geography... arithmetic, or the weary doings of kings and queens.'[3]

He taught himself passages of Shakespeare, Macaulay and Tennyson, which he learned by heart and, like his father, declaimed on his walks in the country round Cranbourne, to Helen's irritation. And perhaps, like the boy in 'The Reluctant Dragon', he 'spent much of his time buried in big volumes that he borrowed from the affable gentry and interested parsons of the country round about'.[4] His siblings considered him intelligent if odd. He read omnivorously, a trait he subsequently – mistakenly – attributed to every young reader.[5]

Mrs Inglis had not brought up her grandchildren in isolation. Before and after the terrible return to Inveraray there were visits from family members, including a younger cousin, Reginald Inglis, who attached himself to Kenneth, disliking Helen and Willie. A fraternity of uncles made forays to Berkshire; Kenneth called them a 'tribe', suggesting savagery. The children's favourite was a commander of HMS *Hercules*, Uncle Jack Inglis, stationed at Plymouth. Mrs Inglis Helen described as 'very sociable'. Social calls were made to and from The Mount and, after, Fern Hill Cottage. Kenneth remembered staid, irksomely formal visits to admire friends' gardens – 'company manners, and perhaps tedious talk of delphiniums and green fly and such'.[6] From cousins, uncles, callers or garden owners, reliable information about school was in short supply. Accounts conflicted. 'According to some it meant larks, revels, emancipation, and a foretaste of the bliss of manhood. According to others... it was a private and peculiar Hades, that could give the original institution points and a beating.'[7] Kenneth would find it a mixture of the two. His description of a new boy at school in an essay called 'The Fairy Wicket' is poignant, redolent of fear: 'his unfledged skin still craving the feathers whereinto he was wont to nestle'.[8]

Afterwards he treated his arrival in this unknown, would-be grown-up environment lightheartedly. There is little doubt that, at the time, 'new kicked out of his nest into the draughty, uncomfortable outer world', the experience unnerved him thoroughly.[9] 'On or about Michaelmas Day 1868, a bright and eager (sullen, reluctant, very ordinary-looking) youth of nine summers sprang lightly (descended reluctantly, was hauled ignominiously) onto the arrival platform of the Great Western Railway Station at Oxford.'[10] In Kenneth's version, it was a solitary test of nerve. It seems likely that Willie, one year his senior and also a pupil at St Edward's, accompanied him. Although Kenneth later referred to the 'rightminded child [that] regarded an elder brother as a veritable god', he excluded Willie from his account, an exercise in rhetorical flourish with an emphasis on his feelings more than a strict record of fact.[11]

By hansom cab – 'extraordinarily shabby... the worst and oldest [hansom] ever seen' – this nervous new boy made the short journey into the middle of Oxford and 'a pleasant, quiet street, central and yet secluded'. New Inn Hall Street connected George Street to Queen Street, a cobbled and unpretentious dogleg of small white gabled cottages, a vicarage and medieval Frewen Hall. Since its founding, St Edward's had occupied Mackworth House, a building leased from Brasenose College that Kenneth estimated at no more than 150 years old; its state of dilapidation was chronic. With characteristic focus on his surrounds, he noted its rickety charm – not so far removed from that of The Mount. In an essay called 'The Spell of Oxford', written at the very end of his life, his descriptions point to picturesqueness: 'a pleasant low wide hall'; 'a low but well-lighted eastward-facing room used as a dining room'; by way of principal schoolroom, in which each boy had a desk of his own, 'a handsome room of some style, running up the full height of the building to a coved ceiling'; 'rabbit-warrenish' bedrooms each home to five or six boys. In 'The Fairy Wicket', written when his memories were sharper, the school is 'barrack-like', the classrooms 'arid, cheerless'.[12]

As he chose to remember it, his first summons was to the masters' sitting room upstairs, overlooking the playground. There, 'a round and rosy young man with side-whiskers...

desired, he said, to record my full name... When he had got it, he tittered girlishly, and murmured "What a *funny* name!"'[13] Kenneth's introduction to headmaster Frederick Fryer, a twentysomething curate of pronounced Oxford Movement leanings, proved equally disconcerting. 'The lowest class, or form, was in session and I was modestly lurking in the lower end of it, wondering what the deuce it was all about, when enter the Headmaster. He did not waste words. Turning to the master in charge of us, he merely said: "If that" (indicating my shrinking figure) "is not up there" (pointing to the upper strata) "by the end of the lesson, he is to be caned." Then like a blast away he passed, and no man saw him more.

'Here was an affair! I was young and tender, well-meaning, not used to being clubbed and assaulted; yet here I was, about to be savaged by big, beefy, hefty, hairy men, called masters! Small wonder that I dissolved into briny tears.'[14]

This description has the polish of a practised anecdote from which any residue of unhappiness has faded with time and repetition, a sign perhaps that the incident was an isolated one. Kenneth's recollections do not suggest that 'briny tears' or fear of assault overwhelmed his schooling, although canings were constant; a friend in his twenties claimed 'he seemed at times as if in his younger days he had been teased, and his boyish aspirations trodden on', an outcome that, with equal probability, can be attributed to his schoolfellows, Uncle John Grahame, Mrs Inglis, or Helen and Willie.[15] Unlike the bulk of his contemporaries at St Edward's, Kenneth had neither mother nor father to miss and scant experience of the conventional childhood 'of lessons, puddings, the embrace maternal, the paternal smack'.[16] His uprooting the previous year from The Mount was every bit as painful a severance as the transition from Cranbourne to New Inn Hall Street, and he had learned already to retreat within himself; his arrival at school was not his first experience of 'a situation... distasteful, out of harmony, jarring'. In the case of the fictional Edward, Kenneth's narrator glimpses on the station platform 'the old order... at its last gasp': Edward's train journey is a metaphor and his initiation into the quasi-adult rites of school will terminate his childhood and the children's easy fellowship.[17] But Kenneth had made his own childhood, escaping into imagination from the triple unhappiness of his mother's death, abandonment by his father and Mrs Inglis's coldness. He may have recognized from the outset St Edward's powerlessness to prevent his emotional and mental absenteeism.

The transition to school was challenging nevertheless for a boy with no father to guide, cajole or instruct him.

St Edward's was chaotic, a 'busy world of rubs and knocks and competition', harum-scarum in its novel unpredictability.[18] The untrained undergraduates, paid as little as £15 a term to teach a narrow curriculum of 'repetitions in Latin, Greek and Latin accidence', took little interest in their charges, and Kenneth would later refer to 'a painfully acquired ignorance of dead languages' and the school's 'lack of care or respect for abstract scholarship'.[19] Physical discomfort was all-encompassing: infestations of rats; rudimentary sanitation; overcrowded dormitories with masters forced to sleep in cupboards; atrocious food; rotten woodwork that led to a floor falling in and splintering banisters; a wall that collapsed into the street. A casual brutality coloured everything, like the headmaster's night-time games of hunting for coins in the dark: 'Ledges in the brick wall were always a favourite hiding place, and lighted touchwood was used as a lantern. Pits were dug and filled with mud and water, and over them, and into them, the unsuspecting ones were lured.'[20]

Such rough and tumble was too much for Willie, whose health was delicate. In 1871 he left St Edward's. Two years earlier, at the beginning of Kenneth's second year, a boy had committed suicide by drowning himself in the river. These cases were exceptional. The majority of the Grahames' schoolmates – in 1869, forty-nine boys aged between eight and eighteen – got by with stubborn endurance, while Kenneth had means of his own of withdrawing in all but body from an unpalatable present. From his own account, he emerges no more or less traumatized than his peers: he even refers to 'those rare white [mornings] at school when it was a whole holiday, and summer was boon and young'.[21] St Edward's diet of frequent beatings did not instil in him habits of particular diligence or obedience. 'Whatever our individual gifts, a general dogged determination to shirk and to evade kept us all at much the same dead level – a level of ignorance tempered by insubordination,' he wrote in a story published in 1895. 'Some few seem to be born without much innate tendency to crime.'[22] His conformity was frequently skin deep.

In place of the typical public school roster of arcane pro- scriptions, for which St Edward's was too new, Kenneth's schooling included unexpected freedoms. So long as they wore school caps, boys were permitted to wander at will about Oxford's cobbled streets. 'It was my chief pleasure to escape at once and foot it here and there, exploring, exploring, always exploring, in a world I had not known the like of before,' Kenneth remembered.[23] He made for 'the stately buildings that clustered round the Radcliffe [Camera]': the Bodleian Library, the colleges of Brasenose and All Souls, the Sheldonian Theatre, with its wrought-iron screen on to Broad Street topped by busts of the twelve Caesars so badly weathered that they resembled 'lumps of black fungoid growth'.[24] He fell in love with the Covered Market, noisy from end to end. In the company of friends he hazarded the shadowy passage of Brasenose Lane. There, according to thrilling schoolboy rumour, after the death of a disreputable drunkard the Devil himself had appeared, 'horned and hoofed and of portentous stature', and extracted 'the wretched man's soul... as a seaside tripper might extract a winkle from its shell with a pin'.[25]

On fine days Kenneth wandered into college gardens: no porter ever queried his right of admission. In the summer after his tenth birthday, he visited St Giles' Fair, a freak show of giants, dwarfs, fat ladies, tattooed ladies, mermaids and 'distorted nature of every variety'. He wandered 'sadly down the row of booths; for my private means would not allow of a closer acquaintance with the interiors', simultaneously absorbed and repelled by the combination of exoticism and 'spoofery' on offer.[26] He returned to the fair regularly. In a canoe, he paddled along reaches of the river, past 'lush meadow-grass, wet orchards, warm, insect-haunted ponds... browsing cattle... haymaking, and... farm-buildings', as far as Osney Lock.[27]

In Oxford he surely first witnessed the spectacle he recorded in an essay called 'Cheap Knowledge'. 'In the long, dark winter evenings, outside some shop window whose gaslight flared brightest into the chilly street, l would see some lad – sometimes even a girl – book in hand, heedless of cold and wet, of aching limbs and straining eyes, careless of jostling passers-by, of rattle and turmoil behind them and about, their happy spirits far in an enchanted world: till the ruthless shopman turned out the gas and brought them rudely back to the bitter reality of cramped legs and numbed fingers.'[28]

To a small boy, craning his neck to gaze, the barred windows and 'massive, bolted and enormous gates' of Oxford's colleges suggested 'Houses of Correction'. Nevertheless, Kenneth was smitten at first sight, their image burned into his fancy. The principal legacy of his schooling would be an enduring romance with Oxford. His abiding memories of St Edward's were concerned not with schoolboys' beastliness or confraternity, but the architecture and environs of the town itself, 'the good grey Gothic on the one hand and, on the other, the cool secluded reaches of the Thames – the "Stripling Thames", remote and dragon-fly haunted', where locks and lock-keepers' gardens inspired dreams in which he 'let the old gates swing, work[ing] the groaning winches, and hear[ing] the water lap and suck and gurgle as it slowly sinks or rises'.[29] In Oxford his absorption in place became a fixed habit.

He did not forge lifelong friendships: companionship was never an urgent requirement. School holidays reunited him with Helen, Willie and Roland. In the summer he and Willie stayed with Uncle Jack Inglis in Portsmouth; they visited Uncle John Grahame in Sussex Gardens, London during the Christmas holidays. His encounters with girls were few, save Helen and Uncle John's daughters Bessie and Agnes mostly restricted to sightings of the girls' school that shared with St Edward's chapel services in the nearby church of St Thomas's. 'Sometimes, trooping down [the road], we contrived for a brief minute to align ourselves with their more formal crocodile, and exchange with it nods... and wreathed smiles. At least we thought we did, though probably these pig-tailed young persons never ever noticed we were there. But we thought they did, and it felt like the dawn of high romance. For everything must have a beginning.'[30] It is a telling recollection. Kenneth's relationships with the opposite sex seldom advanced beyond such uncertain overtures: outside of imagination, he conceived no appetite for high romance, as his wife would discover painfully. At some point in his school career, he knotted a purse out of string, a present presumably intended for a boy's mother. Kenneth gave his purse to Helen, who kept it for sixty years, before bestowing it on Kenneth's widow.

With its education 'of the fine old crusted order,

with all the classics in the top bin', St Edward's inspired Kenneth academically only as a means to an end – his determination, with school over, to remain in Oxford as an undergraduate.[31] To the stately measure of Milton's verse, for example, he responded in a spirit of daydreaming distractedness. His doodles in the margins of *Paradise Lost* included griffins and their traditional enemy, the one-eyed Scythians called Arimaspians. 'What a chance, that Arimaspian, for the imaginative pencil!' he wrote unrepentantly. As with his decorations of Macaulay's *Lays*, doodles remained more firmly in his mind than anything he read: 'And so it has come about that, while Milton periods are mostly effaced from memory by the sponge of Time, I can still see that vengeful Gryphon.'[32]

Instead what Kenneth learned at school was an ability to accommodate himself to prevailing mores, a knack of visible conformity and lip service to majority shibboleths that he would retain: later accounts all commend his solidness of character. So successful was he that he ended as head of school. He acquired a measure of sporting proficiency: captain of the rugby XV, secretary of the cricket 2nd XI. In October 1873, the year the school moved from crumbling Mackworth House to new buildings on Woodstock Road, the *St Edward's School Chronicle* printed his prize-winning essay on the subject of rivalry, a cumbersome rehash of clichés about gentlemanly sportsmanship and Christian kindness, in which he commended 'one of the chief duties of a Christian, to love one another' and the importance of 'contest[ing] with good nature and pleasantness'. Anonymously he submitted livelier, wittier contributions. In the Debating Society he was contrivedly outspoken. There was nothing to choose between Mary I and Elizabeth I, he offered, since 'one was a bigoted Catholic, the other a spiteful Protestant'.[33] He won the sixth form class prize. He won prizes for Latin and divinity, though the school's vigorous Christianity made no more impression than nursery prayers, with the soppy angels he dismissed as 'anaemic, night-gowned nonentities that hovered over the bed of the Sunday-school child in the pages of the *Sabbath Improver*'; he referred to the 'too familiar dowdiness of common places of worship'.[34] He attributed to his time at St Edward's the 'pagan germ' he explored in the rural pantheism of *The Wind in the Willows*.

Kenneth left behind no record of his feelings on leaving school: much later he referred to 'that far-away glow (mingled with self-satisfaction) which I used to feel when I won a prize at school'.[35] He could be forgiven a degree of complacency. His career had outstripped that of his classmates. Reasonably he could claim that he had repaid Uncle John Grahame's modest investment in him. Optimistically he looked to the future and the dream of three more years in Oxford as an undergraduate that had become his lodestar.

It was not to be. John Grahame's plans were quite different. His decision about Kenneth's future countered every assumption his portionless nephew had made. There would be consternation, stinging words – and disappointment from which Kenneth never recovered fully. 'Bitter it is to stumble out of an opalescent dream into the cold daylight,' he stated feelingly.[36] Later he described 'schoolboy hopes... comically misshapen, tawdry and crude in colour'. In the same essay his tone is equivocal. 'Let the pit receive them, and a good riddance!... Let them go. Who cares?... It is time to have done with fancies and get back to a world of facts. If only one could!'[37] Kenneth Grahame's expulsion from Oxford at the hands of his sensible, practical Scottish uncle proved a turning point in his life.

· 4 ·

'The huge world that roars hard by'

WILLIE GRAHAME DIED on the last day of 1874 of pneumonia brought on by bronchial fever. He was sixteen. For Kenneth, it was one more instance of the impermanence of bonds of love and the fragility of family.

His childhood had been shaped by severed relationships: he had lost mother, father and now the sibling closest to him in age. In addition, during his time at St Edward's, Ferguson left Fern Hill Cottage for a situation nearby with a couple called Lidderdale, the daughter and son-in-law of a friend of Mrs Inglis. More than anyone, Ferguson had occupied a parent's role for the Grahame children and invested their upbringing with permanence and continuity. By the time Kenneth left school in the summer of 1875, of the household briefly in the sheriff's house in Inveraray only he, Helen and Roland remained. Helen Grahame had grown into a difficult, exacting young woman, all corners and hard edges. The relationship of brother and sister included its tensions.

Kenneth had no means of rebutting Uncle John Grahame's devastating decision that in place of university he should find employment as soon as possible. Mrs Inglis lived in straitened circumstances: she could offer her grandson no financial assistance, even had she wished to, which is by no means evident. Kenneth was aware of the extent of his dependency. His was a mindset of its time, in which the duty of children towards their elders was a potent force for compliance. Certainly he challenged his uncle. In the face of implacable opposition on the part of this hard-headed Calvinist, Kenneth gave way, as he knew he must.

A decade before, a family council had determined the fate of Bessie Grahame's four motherless children. In 1875, Kenneth's future was decided by the combined efforts of three uncles and his grandmother. It was almost certainly David Inglis's well-meant suggestion that the children continue to visit Ferguson at Ascot Place, which brought Kenneth into contact with his nurse's new employer William Lidderdale – a director, and future governor, of the Bank of England. At some point either Uncle David or Mrs Inglis consulted William Lidderdale about Kenneth's future; Kenneth's quarrel with his favourite uncle many years later probably had its roots in this particular under-taking.[1] Their enquiries elicited an offer of a position at the bank as 'gentleman clerk', as soon as the waiting list permitted. For John Grahame it was the very solution to his dilemma, and he seized upon it. To make good the wait, he offered Kenneth interim employment in the Westminster office of Grahame, Currie and Spens. A third uncle, Robert Grahame, provided accommodation. Draycott Lodge – afterwards home to the pre-Raphaelite painter William Holman Hunt – was a large, old-fashioned, pale-stuccoed villa, with tall windows and urns along the parapet, in still-leafy Fulham. John Grahame also extended a fortnightly invitation to dine in Sussex Gardens on alternate Sundays. Kenneth accepted job, waiting list, new home and invitation. With no alternative he accepted his role as 'palefaced quilldriver'.[2] His uncles' combined efforts had penned him within the family fold, an assertion of Grahame values of respectability, solvency, sobriety. On the surface his childhood was over. In a society that made no concessions to adolescence, at Grahame, Currie and Spens, and despite his overwhelming inexperience, Kenneth would be expected to conduct himself as an adult.

After his death, Kenneth's widow claimed that he was 'always too big for less than a philosophical view of life': his reading at school or shortly after of the *Meditations* of Marcus Aurelius, Roman emperor and Stoic philosopher, sweetened his acquiescence in this avuncular legerdemain concerning his future.[3] He frequently cited the Roman's maxims, his emphasis on 'mental tranquillity, in which alone... lieth the perfection of moral character'.[4] In his published essays Kenneth included quotations from the *Meditations*, including, in 'The Romance of the Road', this striking statement of outward acceptance: 'A man ought to be seen by the gods neither dissatisfied with anything, nor complaining.'[5] An essay called 'Justifiable Homicide' indicates that his own efforts were only partly successful. The essay celebrates an unnamed subject who forestalls the urge to complain by murdering family members. It includes its portion of what looks like wishful thinking. 'Uncles were his special line – (he had suffered much from their tribe, having been early left an orphan)... He possessed (at the beginning of his career) a large number of these connections, and... he always protested (and I believed him) that [pecuniary] gain with him was a secondary consideration.'[6] In a story called 'Dies Irae', written long after disappointment cooled, resignation tempers equanimity: 'Life may be said to be composed of things that come off and things that don't come off.'[7]

Advocacy and accountancy had occupied generations of Grahame men: nothing in the prospect of becoming a gentleman clerk at the Bank of England appealed to sixteen-year-old Kenneth. Although too young to understand it fully, he had witnessed his father's failure in the Argyll judiciary. It was clear to Kenneth, nevertheless, that his own affinities with Cunningham and even Sepulchral Grahame, whom he had not read, were closer than any kinship he felt with steady, sensible, pinchpenny Uncle John. Yet rebellion was impossible. As instinctively conservative as his uncle, Kenneth acknowledged the debt of respect and obedience he owed him. He attributed

John Grahame's opposition to miserliness and was correspondingly angry, but he never seriously considered rejecting his decision. Kenneth's habit of withdrawal from ugly realities – escape into his 'fourth dimension' of imagination, 'this blessed faculty of... a water-tight skin – nay, an armour plating' – was already well developed, his chief emotional defence.[8] With no money of his own and no word from Cunningham Grahame in a decade, he was financially reliant on the uncle with whom he was so badly out of sympathy. His writing suggests that 'the herb called self-heal' – of which he claimed he had 'always a shred or two in his wallet' – offered sustenance of sorts.[9]

He internalized disappointment and revolt. The nature of his feelings emerges in the following decade in the preoccupation in his writing with ideas of avoidance and escape. The university retained its siren allure for Kenneth, but he was entirely powerless to turn dream into reality. In *The Wind in the Willows*, the seafaring rat encourages Rat to run away: '"Take the Adventure, heed the call, now ere the irrevocable moment passes! 'Tis but a banging of the door behind you, a blithesome step forward, and you are out of the old life and into the new!"'[10] In Rat's case, Mole intervenes to stop him. In Kenneth's case, adventure was snatched from his grasp: the door that banged behind him excluded him from the Oxford of his youthful fantasies, with its Gothic spires and calling jackdaws and the slow-moving river he had chartered in a borrowed canoe. Again Kenneth found himself expelled from a private Eden, Uncle John Grahame once more the architect of his unhappiness. 'As a rule... grown-up people are fairly correct on matters of fact; it is in the higher gift of imagination that they are so sadly to seek,' he wrote, bitterly rational, in 1893.[11]

In the autumn of 1875, he departed Cranbourne for London, distant again from the siblings who were his nearest emotional anchor, and entirely friendless. His feelings are not too difficult to conceive.

Over time Kenneth's dislike of London grew. In his sixties, he would claim that the ideal London was that sketched by Daisy Ashford in *The Young Visiters*, 'mainly a compound of the Crystal Palace' – which Kenneth loved and visited repeatedly – 'and the private apartments at Hampton Court, lightly tricked out with an hotel, a hansom-cab and a policeman'.[12] His mistrust of urban life, with its squalor and poverty and the sooty drudgery of mechanization, was a commonplace of the age: it inspired, among others, William Morris and his vision of a rural paradise. Kenneth's response, characteristically, was not a craving for reform but detachment and a longing for absence. Among his jottings from his first years in the capital was a single stanza of Matthew Arnold's 'Lines Written in Kensington Garden':

In the huge world, which roars hard by,
Be others happy if they can!
But in my helpless cradle I
Was breathed on by the rural Pan.[13]

Later he borrowed from Arnold's verse the title of an essay, 'The Rural Pan', in which he explored a schism between man and nature that he attributed to industrialization and the growth of towns. He described first exposure to London, 'the clatter and roar of its ceaseless wheels', as 'portentous, terrifying, nay, not to be endured'.[14]

He found crumbs of comfort at Draycott Lodge. A generation earlier, market gardens, nut trees and fruit growing had dominated swathes of Fulham, Kensington and Earl's Court. In Uncle Robert Grahame's house, whispers of this semi-rural past lingered. Robert's wife Georgina shared Kenneth's engagement with landscape. The couple had lived until recently in Manila; they leased 'a little old farm-house' in Italy. Georgina Grahame's descriptions of her garden at the Villino Landau near Florence, published anonymously in *In a Tuscan Garden* in 1902, are sensuously picturesque. Kenneth walked to the offices of Grahame, Currie and Spens along the banks of the Thames or through the crowded, shabby streets of Soho, where, like Georgina Grahame's Tuscan reminiscences, cheap Italian restaurants hinted at the rich, earthy, pungent pleasures of the South, inveigling Kenneth into solitary suppers and another line of escapist reverie. He made detours via Trafalgar Square to the National Gallery, attracted by 'a little "St Catherine" by Pinturicchio that possessed my undivided affections', a picture hung so low on the gallery walls 'that those who would worship' – Kenneth among them – 'must grovel'.[15] He looked at paintings by father and son Filippo and Filippino Lippi and the *Fiesole San Domenico Altarpiece* attributed to Fra Angelico, influenced in his appreciation by John Ruskin's writing on Italian Primitives. He recycled the experience in 'The Iniquity of Oblivion', his story of a stockbroker 'steeping his soul' in early Italian art and exchanging commercial London for 'the full sunlight that steeps the Lombard plain'.[16] In the square outside the gallery Kenneth delighted in the street artist 'portraying [in chalks] with passionate absorption, the half of a salmon on a plate; with special attention to the flesh-tints at the divided part'. Contentedly he watched the flocks of 'pigeons flash and circle, joyous as if they sped their morris over some remote little farmstead, lapped round by quiet hills... the sunlight fall[ing] off their wings in glancing drops of opal sheen'.[17] His descriptions reduce the life of the city to a series of vivid magic lantern slides. Kenneth is an observer. He admires the spectacle that he edits visually, even as he watches it, and his chief admiration is reserved for reflections of the country.

Also in Draycott Lodge lived Robert and Georgina Grahame's only daughter Annie. Close in age, the cousins would gradually become friends, hampered at first by Kenneth's diffidence and reserve and his absences from Fulham during working hours, but drawn together by shared interests. In June 1877, at Kenneth's suggestion, both became members of the New Shakspere Society (sic). Three months later, they holidayed in Pitlochry with Uncle John Grahame, his children Agnes and Walter, and Helen and Roland. Annie 'had been reared on old Scotch ballads and stories and folklore', the very stuff of Mrs Inglis's mothering. In Pitlochry, as summer gave way to autumn's shortening days, ballads and stories and folklore played their part in the fireside home entertainment these mid-Victorians relished. This 'appealed to Kenneth', Annie remembered, as indeed it would.[18] 'Later on at any rate [it] formed a bond of union between us,' she added, vague about the nature of that union. All his life Kenneth appreciated the colour and vim of fairy tales: their turbulent narratives preserved a connection with that vibrant world of boyhood he would not relinquish. In Pitlochry, in the stuccoed villa in Fulham, in the soot and grime of London, Annie's Scottish stories, complete with fairies and magic, recalled Kenneth to his west coast infancy and the trouble-free years on the banks of Loch Fyne before his mother's death and the awful shadow of his father's weakness; they forged a link with the best years at The Mount and his grandmother's storytelling.

On a young man in imaginative retreat from disappointment, Annie's Scottish folklore doubtless made a strong impression. Communicated much later to Kenneth's first biographer, Patrick Chalmers, Annie's memories seem to point to affection between the cousins, and it is possible that, at Draycott Lodge, chastely and tentatively, Annie Grahame became Kenneth's first love. Suggestively, Kenneth's widow Elspeth excluded any mention of Annie from Chalmers's biography written during her own lifetime.[19] For her part, Annie never married. Meanwhile Kenneth inventoried the onset of love in conventional fashion. His description reveals no more than a generalized familiarity with the tremors of obsession: 'There is the first sight of the Object, accompanied by a catching of the breath, a trembling in the limbs, loss of appetite, ungovernable desire, and a habit of melancholy in secret places.'[20]

With apparent equanimity, Kenneth applied himself to office life. The exact nature of his work at Grahame, Currie and Spens was vague, even to his family. Outside the office, he began teaching himself shorthand. Uncle John Grahame commended his diligence as 'pluck and steadiness' and discouraged the shorthand. Inspired by office talk of politics and politicians, Kenneth briefly aspired to political journalism. John Grahame scented danger. He suggested the equivalent of the Territorial Army. Once again Kenneth did not demur. He joined a recently formed volunteer infantry regiment, the London Scottish. Drill, boxing and fencing took the place of shorthand. St Edward's had served to institutionalize him. It would be a mistake to consider this sort of toy-soldiering anathema to him, but in the surviving photograph of Kenneth in his London Scottish uniform, his expression is more than usually guarded, his recoil from the camera more than usually striking.

At St Edward's Kenneth had learned to negotiate the conflicting claims of 'imagination... in healthy working order', with its colourful vistas into other worlds, and the diktats of conventional expectation.[21] Immurement at Grahame, Currie and Spens exacerbated this disconnect between inner romanticism and conformity on the surface. In private Kenneth began to write. Writing poetry had been

Helen's response to Cunningham's collapse, following her final months with her father in Inveraray. It is Mole's remedy for Rat's wanderlust in *The Wind in the Willows*: "'It's quite a long time since you did any poetry," [Mole] remarked. "You might have a try at it this evening – instead of, well, brooding over things so much. I've an idea that you'll feel a lot better when you've got something jotted down – if it's only just the rhymes."'[22] Kenneth's writing took the form of a handful of anonymous contributions to the *St Edward's School Chronicle*. Proof that, like Rat, it did indeed make him feel better, once begun, he would write on and off for the next two decades.

'To him who is destined to arrive, the fates never fail to afford, on the way, their small encouragements,' Kenneth wrote optimistically in 1895.[23] In his own case, encouragement came in the leonine form of irascible savant Frederick Furnivall. Furnivall was a literary zealot, a philologist, an editor of the *New English Dictionary*, founder of the Early English Text Society, the Chaucer Society, the Ballad Society and the New Shakspere Society. Like Kenneth, he kept faith lifelong with his boyhood enthusiasms: in Furnivall's case, an absorption in medieval literature begun when, as a child, he read Tennyson's *Morte d'Arthur*. He was a

Christian Socialist who taught grammar at the Working Men's College, a barrister who practised intermittently as a conveyancer, a sculling enthusiast who badgered most of his friends onto the river. In equal measure he inspired discipleship and hostility.

Kenneth met Furnivall in Soho, in an Italian restaurant some time in 1876. At first glance they had little in common, the gauche seventeen-year-old and this pugnacious dynamo, thirty-four years his senior, who cocked a snook at convention in ways Kenneth never would, with his idiosyncratic dress and bold, outspoken conversation and behaviour. Furnivall was at the centre of a crowded table, Kenneth on his own. Their introduction was informal – laughter on Kenneth's part, overhearing one of Furnivall's anecdotes, then an exchange of cards. It would be the first of many meetings. And it was to Furnivall, eminently well connected in literary London, that Kenneth would first show his writing.

· 5 ·

'Journeymen in this great whirling London mill'

'To know what you would like to do is one thing,' Kenneth wrote in 1892. 'To go out boldly and do it is another – and a rarer.'[1]

On 1 January 1879, in line with the wishes of his family, Kenneth arrived for the first time at the Bank of England and the position of gentleman clerk secured for him by William Lidderdale. He was nineteen years old, serious-minded, tall, broad-shouldered, no longer a child. In recent examinations for bank entry he had been awarded full marks for written composition for the only time in the bank's history: an essay on the subject of India. He was greeted not by laurels, but the thickest yellow fog of the winter, so heavy over Threadneedle Street that the bulk of the bank's employees had stayed away. His own short journey, from a new rented flat in Bloomsbury Street – the first home he could call his own – had taken him an hour and a half through impenetrable murk.

Prudent John Grahame could not have made a safer choice for the nephew he did not understand than clerical work in the City. By the early 1870s, London's financial institutions employed more than 120,000 frock-coated, stiff-white-collared clerks to write out by hand the invoices, letters and ledger entries of Victorian Britain's trading revolution. In the Bank of England, a clerk's position was for life, with no compulsory retirement age. On the surface,

John Grahame's certainty that he had found the answer for an educated, socially privileged young man without means was persuasive.

Kenneth kept to himself any misgivings he retained; exigency and compulsion seldom win hearts and minds. In *Twice Round the Clock; or the Hours of the Day and Night in London*, published in 1859, George Augustus Sala had painted a sober picture of the clerk's working day. He described a 'great army of clerk martyrs... [setting] down their loads of cash-book and ledger-fillers' each morning like clockwork. He apostrophized their wretchedness: 'What an incalculable mass of figures must be collected in those commercial heads!... What a chaos of cash debtor, contra creditor, bills payable and bills receivable; waste-books, day-books, cash-books and journals; insurance policies and brokerage, dock warrants and general commercial bedevilment.'[2]

At intervals Kenneth would indeed come to consider himself a 'clerk martyr'. Rejection of commercial, corporate and committee life peppers his writing. Essays including 'The Eternal Whither', 'A Bohemian in Exile', 'Long Odds' and 'Orion' celebrate the 'escape' of city men from daily grind: the 'old cashier in some ancient City establishment whose practice was to spend his yearly holiday in relieving some turnpike-man at his post'; Fothergill, who 'passed out of our lives by way of the Bayswater Road' for the north Berkshire Downs, a cart, a mare, 'a few canvases and other artists' materials'; the secretary of 'some venerable Company or Corporation dating from Henry VII', who 'sent in his resignation, and with comfortable pension... crossed the Channel and worked South till he came to Venice' and the Lido and a seahorse washed up on the sand; the stockbroker with a villa and a steam launch at Surbiton found tickling trout 'in a wild nook of Hampshire'.[3] In his satirical story of a seventeenth-century executioner, 'The Headswoman', Kenneth presents the town council as archetypal in its 'general absence of any characteristic at all – unless a pervading hopeless insignificance can be considered as such'; in the same story he dismisses legalities as 'a mass of lies, quibbles, dodges and tricks'.[4] This was the world that Cunningham had rejected: Kenneth's acceptance was equally qualified. Even long after his retirement, he rebuffed a suggestion that he write a magazine article about his experiences at the bank with the firm 'Nothin' Doin' about B. of E [Bank of England]. Much too dull a subject.'[5]

Kenneth's childhood happiness – those intense solitary dream adventures set against the backdrop of The Mount – had been achieved in the face of bereavement, his father's rejection and Mrs Inglis's stern distractedness. In John

Grahame's Westminster offices, he had toyed with thoughts of political journalism: the dream shattered, he himself was not destroyed. Of his life lessons to date, none had been repeated so often as the pragmatism of adaptability. On the surface, as it would remain, pragmatism rather than rebellion was uppermost in Kenneth's nature; and pragmatism did not preclude enjoyment. He remained at the Bank for England for thirty years, although two of his published essay collections, *The Golden Age* and *Dream Days*, were bestsellers and his wife an heiress. Save that brief hankering for political journalism, he never aspired to write full time.

His response to City life was not, as might be expected and has sometimes been suggested, one of wretchedness and outright rejection. At times the Bank of England bored him. Then, as in his essay 'The Rural Pan', 'through shady Throgmorton Street and about the vale of Cheapside the restless Mercury [flitted], with furtive eye and voice a little hoarse', the restless Mercury an image of Kenneth's distraction.[6] At other times he enjoyed the bank's venerable kaleidoscope: dividend day and shareholders of every shape, size and, apparently, level of neediness; the patrol of nightwatchmen with their lanterns, like an historical pageant; bullion vaults stacked like baker's shelves with bars of silver and gold, and the slender bank cats chasing mice through lofty chambers. He enjoyed the methodical repetitions of clerical work, long chophouse lunches and errands that took him near and far, crisscrossing the capital. Like George the clerk in Jerome K. Jerome's *Three Men in a Boat*, 'who goes to sleep at a bank from ten to four each day', he enjoyed the rhythm of short, unhurried working days – one day, according to a surviving scrap of diary, he departed the bank at eleven o'clock in the morning, his work completed. In time, he enjoyed the freedom to decide for himself his comings and goings. He enjoyed the bank's entrenched traditionalism. 'If we are perfectly honest with ourselves,' he wrote in 1921, 'we must admit that we always do the thing that we really like doing, for the sake of the doing itself.'[7] For much of the time, he was as numb to the unsympathetic aspects of bank life as he had become to the blows of his childhood and the brutishness of St Edward's. 'To all of us journeymen in this great whirling London mill, it happens sooner or later that the clatter and roar of its ceaseless wheels... becomes a part of our nature, with our clothes and our acquaintances,' he wrote, 'till at last the racket and din of a competitive striving humanity... cease to impinge on the sense,' leaving him undisturbed with the absorbing inner life with which he consistently sought to shield himself.[8] By 1879, for as long as he could remember, Kenneth had led a double life, slipping between the workaday world and wellsprings of rich fantasy. Employment at the Bank of England, like St Edward's and the years of disillusionment at Grahame, Currie and Spens, consolidated this habit of mental dualism. Boredom and incomprehension opened doors into other realms.

Unexpectedly in his favour was the bank's affinity with the rumbustious lost world of the 'Gallery' and the games played at The Mount with Helen, Willie and the infant Roland. Kenneth's arid preconceptions of the bank were shaped by Uncle John Grahame and whatever childish impressions he himself had formed at Ascot Place of William Lidderdale; he had not anticipated an environment of any imaginative appeal. In the event, the Bank of England astonished him. He would discover that its multiple identities were every bit as surprising as his own.

'Gentlemen' clerks were frequently anything but. The loutish hurly-burly of junior bank staff startled this reserved, self-contained young man whose social exposure had been narrow. Among its lower echelons, as a contemporary of Kenneth's recorded, the bank was a rowdy pandemonium of pranks and 'flying Pass-books' and 'the singing of a line from some popular song winding up with "Amen" in a solemn cadence of about a hundred voices'.[9] Employees were regularly so drunk that they were forced to lie down on tables to recover. Animal carcases were deposited in lavatories awaiting amateur butchery at the end of the day. In cloakrooms after hours, wagers were laid on illicit dog fights. Clerks brawled and spat. The impression is of a Hogarthian cockfighting den. Fastidious Kenneth observed with horrified fascination – and combed the bank's official records for past instances of unruliness or eccentricity, like the story of the clerk-turned-turnpike-man that he recycled in 'The Eternal Whither' or the abrupt termination of employment of an unnamed predecessor, who 'did not attend at his office today, having been hanged at eight o'clock in the morning for horse-stealing'.[10] Topsy-turvily an elderly Scottish ledger clerk criticized the neat regularity of Kenneth's handwriting: 'It's no' the hand of a principal, young Grahame.'[11]

A measure of financial independence was Kenneth's short-term reward, as John Grahame had intended, although bank salaries of the time were modest. Kenneth kept careful accounts, shrewd in every aspect of financial management, and would continue to do so. Predictably, bank life satisfied only a fraction of his thoughts. At Grahame, Currie and Spens, he had submitted mannered contributions to the *St Edward's School Chronicle*, perhaps with the purpose of persuading his unbending uncle to reconsider the possibility of a career in journalism. From first arrival in Threadneedle Street, Kenneth devoted non-working hours to writing. He purloined a bank ledger for the purpose; alongside his own efforts were scraps of Horace, Caxton's *Golden Legend* and poetry by Robert Herrick. His membership of Furnivall's New Shakspere Society was a settled thing. Since 1877, he had acted as the society's honorary secretary, present at its monthly meetings in rooms at University College – silent mostly, according to the society's minutes; a watcher, witness to Furnivall's boisterous charisma, his enthusiasms, his peppery tracasseries. The tug of Furnivall and literary London was well established by the time Kenneth entered his apprentice clerkship: his loyalty to the bank was as circumscribed as his faithfulness to John Grahame's vision of family respectability. He kept up his membership of the London Scottish, changing into uniform before departure from Threadneedle Street. After 1884, again at Furnivall's prompting, he helped out at Toynbee Hall in Stepney, organizing sing-songs, billiards and boxing for young East Enders, while recent graduates from Oxford and Cambridge provided lectures. At the neighbouring Whitechapel Art Gallery, part of the same philanthropic foundation, he saw exhibitions of modern art: Millais, Watts, Alma-Tadema, Burne-Jones; in a story written later he satirized Burne-Jones's style: 'vapid, colourless, uninteresting characters, with straight up-and-down sort of figures, white night-gowns, white wings, and the same straight yellow hair parted in the middle'.[12] None of the artists' work moved him to the extent of future encounters with early Italian or Flemish painting. For relaxation he visited the popular Turkish baths, drawn by their promise of 'a certain supernal, deific, state of mind... [a] golden glow of the faculties', part opiate, part hallucination.[13]

For a decade Kenneth did not allow himself any return to Oxford, save to visit his cousin Reginald Inglis at St Edward's. Instead he repeatedly dreamed of the city, 'the real thing, yet transformed and better, because the Gothic was better – a maze of lovely cloisters and chapels and courts', proof of Oxford's enduring stranglehold on his imagination and the impact on him of reading John Ruskin's 'The Nature of Gothic' in *The Stones of Venice*.[14] Characteristically, his dreams had the tendency to make Kenneth happy. Awake, he had the bank and first tentative exercises in writing and, in the flat in Bloomsbury Street, a space in which to indulge the fantasies of home that balanced his longing for escape.

In *The Wind in the Willows*, in Badger's large, fire-lit kitchen, 'rows of spotless plates winked from the shelves of the dresser... The ruddy brick floor smiled up at the smoky ceiling; the oaken settles, shiny with long wear, exchanged cheerful glances with each other; plates on the dresser grinned at pots on the shelf, and the merry firelight flickered and played over everything without distinction.'[15] In Kenneth's description, inanimate objects betray human impulses and emotions, animism he would also apply to landscape and even weather.[16] Home – in Badger's case a 'safe anchorage' of 'embracing light and warmth' – assumes the parent's role of security and protection that Kenneth had missed under Mrs Inglis's roof. It is these attributes he sought out, and imposed upon, the places he chose to live himself.

The flat in Bloomsbury Street lay within convenient walking distance of the bank. At twenty-five shillings, its weekly rent represented a considerable outlay for a junior clerk. As much as 'safe anchorage', it provided him with a space in which to enjoy autonomy that was more than imaginary. His enjoyment was brief. At some point before 1882, Roland followed Kenneth to the Bank of England. He followed him to Bloomsbury Street too, using the flat's sitting room as his bedroom, an arrangement untenable beyond the short term.

Before Roland's advent, Kenneth embraced the joy of sole possession by arranging the flat entirely to his own liking – as he once described his ideal interior, 'little rooms, full of books and pictures, and clean of the antimacassar taint'.[17] His domestic routines were his own, too – a fussy way of making coffee from freshly ground beans using an earthenware strainer, evening pipes of Honeydew tobacco, the ash knocked out on the fire grate, carefully in the case of his favourite long clay pipes. Friends commended his 'very good taste and... great appreciation of beautiful things', the thoughtful placing of a piece of furniture found in an antiques shop or junkshop.[18] He visited sales rooms, coveting woodcuts and etchings; in bookshops, in place of 'the two-and-sixpenny edition for the million', he coveted the latest 'volume of poems in large paper'.[19] The intensity of his quest for home and his preoccupation with its orderly appearance and workings were legacies of his peripatetic childhood, with its frequent dispossessions of place and person. As years before he had dreamed repeatedly of a cream-coloured pony with a long-flowing tail, a vision of an ideal room came to dominate Kenneth's dreams. 'A certain little room very dear and familiar', this dream room impressed upon him 'a sense of snugness, of cushioned comfort, of home-coming', like the rooms he provides for Mole, Rat and Badger. 'All was modest – O, so very modest! But all was my very own, and, what was more, everything in that room was exactly right.'[20] To a sympathetic friend he described the room he saw in his sleep. He also described a waking game he played with himself, of walking London's streets in pursuit of this imaginary space that he had determined *must* exist. His need for its reality – or for proof of the reality of his dream – was a marker of the extent of his longing for 'the well-known staircase... the ever-welcoming door... the same feeling of a homecoming'. The room contained a fire and 'the most comfortable chair in the world' – like Badger's kitchen, where Badger, Rat and Mole 'gathered round the glowing embers of the great wood fire, and thought how jolly it was to be sitting up *so* late, and *so* independent'.[21] Far from feeling disappointment at his failure to locate the room in fact, Kenneth celebrated its 'enchanting possibility' and continued to dream of it.[22]

At weekends he returned to the country he knew, walking or rowing that stretch of the Thames that links Cookham Dean to Cranbourne and beyond in both directions – as far once as Blewbury, close to Didcot, where on Mr Caudwell's farm he saw a row of rats nailed to a wooden door, genesis of one of his darker essays, 'The Barn Door'. He set off from the Thames-side village of Streatley to explore the Ridgeway, following 'a broad green ribbon of turf' that sliced through an 'almost trackless expanse of billowy Downs', eventually reaching Cuckhamsley Hill, some 10 miles distant. Like the shepherd in 'The Reluctant Dragon', 'up on the wide ocean-bosom of the Downs, with only the sun and the stars and the sheep for company, and the friendly chattering world of men and women far out of sight and hearing', he exulted in the sheer size and emptiness of the landscape.[23] He pictured himself 'alone with the southwest wind and the blue sky' as if his surrounds had absorbed him bodily, he himself a part of nature's huge panoply; and he insisted on his place in the sweeping panorama, noticing the 'sky that was always dancing, shimmering, softly talking', listening to 'the water's own noises'.[24]

In a boat with a single paddle, he drifted downstream, glimpsing loosestrife and meadowsweet and flowering bulrushes at the water's edge. Minutely he traced the coming of spring, 'the thrust of the snowdrop and then the crocus, the first green thrill that passes through the quickset hedgerows, the tender wash of faint water-colour that tells of the winter wheat coming thrusting through, the touch of rosiness in the black elm tree-tops'.[25] He observed whatever was immutable, unchanging, dependable, features that allowed him to move at will from the present into his imagining of the past. At sunset he retreated to a 'rustic inn', armed always with tobacco and his pipe, ready for chops and ale and the promise of 'the surest and the sweetest sleep'.[26] His week fell into unequal halves, separated by location. The divide expressed the split in Kenneth himself. It was the country that engaged him viscerally and emotionally. He would evolve a theory that 'there were two Englands existing together, the one firing the great iron highways wherever they might go... the other, unguessed at by many, in whatever places were still vacant of shriek and rattle... the England of heath and common and windy sheep down, of by-lanes and village-greens'.[27] Conservative Kenneth endowed this 'other', older England with virtues: honesty, harmony, beauty. He escaped the 'shriek and rattle' in the Downs' ancient still-nesses – and in imagination and, over time, in his own writing. Wish fulfilment played its part in his outlook. His nostalgia for an idealized countryside had a political dimension, implicitly an endorsement of age-old rural hierarchies and the dominance of a landowning class to which he did not belong. From Monday to Friday, according to Dame Henrietta Barnett, who encountered him at Toynbee Hall, he 'seemed outwardly but a young City man with a dutiful consideration for his poorer neighbours'.[28]

In London, the company of Furnivall and his coterie or family members, and his evenings with the London Scottish, still left time for reading. Beginning in 1878, Smith, Elder & Co published collections of Richard Jefferies's natural history articles for the *Pall Mall Gazette*. Kenneth cannot have known at the time the debt he would incur to Jefferies's subsequent children's stories, *Wood Magic* and

Bevis, in which a child communicates with the elements and animals – a talking mouse, rat and weasel – and the writer explores without sentiment a boy's imagination.

By his early twenties, Kenneth had acquired a gloss of sophistication. He dressed smartly, even to the point of dandyism, a camellia his preferred buttonhole. A friend of Helen's described 'a tall... fine-looking young man, a splendid head, broad and well-proportioned'; she noted his 'large, widely opened rather light grey eyes, always with a kindly expression in them... sensitive hands and mouth'.[29] A clipped crescent of moustache marked the transition from boyhood; already his hair was beginning to thin. At home he was seldom far from his pipe. In an essay on smoking, he called tobacco 'the true Herb of Grace, and a joy and healing balm, and respite and nepenthe'; he dismissed cigarettes as 'shadows of the substance'.[30] To Reginald Inglis he remained a favourite cousin. Kenneth took the impressionable sixteen-year-old to the theatre, to supper in Soho, a little Italian restaurant offering 'about ten courses for 1s. 6d'; he offered him nightcaps of whisky and hot water and a favourite clay pipe that Reginald broke in his nervousness. Reginald observed Kenneth and Roland's bachelor independence, including, it seems, undercurrents of tension between them. He recorded Kenneth's variable health. Physically Kenneth had never completely recovered from the scarlet fever he had caught from Bessie Grahame at the age of five; he suffered bronchial problems and recurrent bouts of 'what they called in those days inflammation of the bowels', so severe on one occasion that his life appeared in danger. His convalescence involved lengthy, not unwelcome, absences from the bank.[31] Either Reginald noticed for himself, or Kenneth told him, that he had begun submitting unsolicited contributions 'to magazines and some literary pages'.[32]

It was Furnivall who encouraged his writing. With some trepidation, Kenneth had shown him the bank ledger he filled with commonplaces, essays written under the combined influence of Robert Louis Stevenson and *Punch*, and poetry. The ledger disappeared following the death of Kenneth's widow: all that survive are extracts quoted in 1933 by Patrick Chalmers. The poetry, as preserved in Chalmers's extracts, is vapid even at its most pessimistic, and cumbrously metrical; the prose is sprightlier, though preoccupied by 'harrying troubles' and a sense of failure.[33] Furnivall advised Kenneth to concentrate on prose. That he treated the younger man so gently points to affectionate esteem as well as perceptiveness. Similar feelings had prompted his invitation that Kenneth take on the secretaryship of the New Shakspere Society a year after they met.

In 1882 or thereabouts, Kenneth left the flat in Blooms-bury Street. He moved – without Roland – to a waterside eyrie. His roof-top flat at 65 Chelsea Gardens, his home until 1894, lay at the top of winding spirals of stone stairs, 'like climbing the stairs of a lighthouse' in one view or, more prosaically, 'interminable dingy stairs'.[34] To Kenneth's contemporaries, Chelsea was riparian, bohemian, artistic, damp, transgressive. To Kenneth it offered views over the Thames and, beyond, broad green expanses of Battersea Park, and at sunset, clouds 'massing themselves in a low violet bank [and] to north and south, as far round as eye could reach, a narrow streak of gold [that] stretched away, straight along the horizon'.[35] By ferry-steamer boarded at Chelsea Embankment, he travelled back and forth to the Bank of England. At least once he 'got up at 6, and went a delightful walk by the river before breakfast'.[36]

Georgina Grahame helped the motherless young man with his domestic arrangements. In the window a gate-legged tea table overlooked the river. A Chippendale bureau bought inexpensively in the Portobello Road and rum-oured to have belonged to the Duke of Wellington revealed a hidden compartment that later inspired Kenneth's story

'The Secret Drawer', in which a 'faint odour of orris-root...
seemed to identify itself with the yellows and browns of
the old wood' and, at last, 'with a sort of small sigh, almost a
sob – as it were – of relief, the secret drawer sprang open'.[37]
In Kenneth's story, the drawer discloses 'a real boy's hoard':
buttons from a sailor's uniform, foreign copper coins, 'a
list of bird's eggs, with names of the places where they had
been found... a ferret's muzzle, and a twist of tarry string,
still faintly aromatic'.[38] To a visitor to the flat, Kenneth
revealed his disappointment that the real secret drawer
probably contained no more than the duke's love letters.
His replacement of these with boyish treasure trove in his
story is characteristic. Avoidance of the subject of adult
relationships was already a firm habit, as it is with the
would-be writer-hero of E. M. Forster's novel *The Longest
Journey*, published in 1907, who announces 'My notion
just now is to leave the passions on the fringe.'[39] (Kenneth
shared a number of traits with Forster's Rickie Elliot: self-
effacement and sensitivity, awkwardness in his relations
with women – the limitations of an over-rigid classical
education.) In time, over everything, as Kenneth described
rooms belonging to a fictional clergyman, 'a faint aroma
of tobacco cheered and heartened exceedingly'.[40] He either
cooked for himself or went out for meals. No accounts
mention anywhere in the flat reminders of his parents.

Amid the roof-tops in Chelsea Gardens, although he entertained cousins and colleagues from the bank there, Kenneth found opportunities for the solitude that, in the welcome absence of binding emotional ties, had become a necessity to him. The flat's cool grey light, reflected off the river, was entirely conducive to the somnolence in which he daydreamed. In surroundings he had fashioned for himself he found reassurance and tangible happiness, like Mole at Mole End: 'ere he closed his eyes he let them wander round his old room, mellow in the glow of the firelight that played or rested on familiar and friendly things which had long been unconsciously a part of him, and now smilingly received him back'.[41] Possessions and the act of possessing buoyed his spirits: 'a brooding sense of peace and of possession' dominates his account of his dream of the perfect room. Like Mole, in thought if not in action, he 'needs must go and caress his possessions'; he was reassured by 'this place which was all his own, these things which were so glad to see him again and could always be counted upon for the same simple welcome'.[42] His writing suggests that his reaction to overwhelming unhappiness as a child had been 'mental aloofness – [the] habit of withdrawal into a secret chamber, of which [the child] sternly guards the key' or into secret adventures of his own devising.[43] The top-floor flat in which he lived alone for a dozen years was one more 'secret chamber'. In a personal life of limited emotional scope, cherished surrounds provided a sense of belonging and wholeness of sorts.

Nevertheless, another six years would pass before Kenneth's writing appeared in print. 'By a Northern Furrow', the first of his paeans to the Berkshire Downs, was published anonymously in the *St James's Gazette* in December 1888.

· 6 ·

'The memory of the glades and wood'

IN HIS MID-TWENTIES, before his writing found its own voice, Kenneth made a series of formative journeys that redrew the boundaries of his imagination.

His first visit to Cornwall, in August 1884, in the company of his sister Helen, was prompted by illness. The siblings travelled to the Lizard peninsula, England's southernmost tip, all but surrounded by the sea. Helen had become a hospital nurse, practical and capable, confirmed in her spinsterhood. A quality in her that Kenneth called her awkwardness was at odds with his own irresolute dreamy withdrawal from unpleasantness: she was vigilant and attentive in her care for him. Brother and sister stayed in a cottage belonging to Helen's friend Mary Richardson.

Distance from London and sea air wrought their magic on Kenneth; he was always susceptible to 'the feel of the warm sun striking hard between my shoulder-blades'.[1] At The Mount, he had revelled in 'treasures of hedge and ditch; the rapt surprise of the first lords-and-ladies, the rustle of a field-mouse, the splash of a frog'.[2] Thrilled by 'the wildness, freshness and strangeness of the Lizard, its grandeur and sparkling air', and with his illness on the wane, he rediscovered the sea.[3] He had been too young for boats at Ardrishaig and Inveraray; but here, for a second time, Kenneth encountered a community dependent on the sea's harvest. Inevitably he took a rosy view of the way of life, remote from any urban centre and the ugly, impersonal, mechanized stamp of 'progress' that he blamed for banishing 'the old enchantment' elsewhere: 'the colliery, the leprosy of suburban brickfields, the devastating network which the railway spider ejects'.[4]

In Cornwall in 1884, Kenneth went native. He spent as much of his time as possible among the fishermen, until his hair was streaked with lighter brown and his face sunburned. Like the wayfaring rat in *The Wind in the Willows*, he adopted the fishermen's dress of 'knitted jersey... of a faded blue, breeches, patched and stained... based on a blue foundation... and a blue cotton handkerchief' and was delighted when a holidaying don from Oxford mistook him for a local.[5] He ate like a native too: leek pasties wrapped in hot flannels to keep them warm; stargazy pie, in which whole pilchards poke head first through golden pastry; rolls of new bread split open and filled with clotted cream; and slices of warm bread spread with cream and drizzled with zigzags of treacle, called 'Thunder and Lightning'. Mary Richardson noted that ordinarily Kenneth was 'distinctly reserved'.[6] Among the fisherfolk, his standoffishness evaporated.

One thrilling night he joined the crew of the local lifeboat, when a White Star liner carrying frozen meat was wrecked offshore. The meat had been wrapped in sheepskins: the skins floated while the meat sank, boon for the fishermen and more valuable than their usual haul. Kenneth learned to catch cod, pollock, mackerel and sardines and, in the early evening, in the shadowy dusk of late summer, by lugger lamp fished for conger eels in the deep water beyond the harbour. He joked afterwards that, only once a 25-pound conger eel had made it into the boat, did the fun really begin. Sometimes he fished all night, in a boat belonging to an elderly fisherman called Tom Roberts. Through unhurried days he immersed himself in a version of those outdoor games of his imagining, his mind recasting each boisterous new escapade as an incident in stories he had read by Ballantyne or, more recently, *Treasure Island*. Like the boy heroes of fiction, in Cornwall he lived in an eternal present, with no mind for the return to London and the workaday world. Impressions silted into memory, dredged up later: 'the hungry complaint of the gulls and the sea-mews, the soft thunder of the breaking wave, the cry of the protesting shingle', as the seafaring rat describes them to Rat. 'Of deep-sea fishings he heard tell, and mighty silver gatherings of the mile-long net; of sudden perils, noise of breakers on a moonlit night... the splash of the hawser'.[7] In local bric-à-brac shops, Kenneth acquired the first of a large collection of the painted glass rolling pins called Sailor's Farewells traditionally given by sailors to their sweethearts. He bought Nailsea glass and

Battersea enamels. They would find their place among the careful arrangements of the attic flat.

His first experience of Italy was with his cousin Annie Grahame in 1886. The hillside farmhouse leased by Annie's parents, 'in a large park bordered by beautiful old ilexes and fir trees, with splendid conifers, tulip-trees and catalpas planted here and there', overlooked nearby Florence and, in the distance, the hills of Vallombrosa and the Apennine mountains.[8] In Georgina Grahame's well-ordered Italian garden, Kenneth encountered verdancy undreamed of at The Mount. Over the courtyard hung the scent of lemon trees; there were tall stems of Madonna lilies with their flecked white trumpet flowers and heady perfume, roses and scented narcissi and festoons of climbing jasmine. Inside, Mrs Grahame had commissioned stencilled wall decoration 'in artistic designs, copied from old Italian brocades'. She installed servants' bells and terracotta fireplaces and, for good measure, 'had several pieces of old English silver standing on shelves in the dining room'. In such beguiling surrounds, so different from the 'gloomy squares and dusty streets' of London, their exoticism tempered by service bells and family silver, Kenneth could be simultaneously inspired and cosseted.[9]

The trip to Italy was a retreat from scandal. The previous year, Furnivall had founded the Shelley Society. At the Grand Theatre, Islington, on 7 May 1886, in front of an audience that included George Bernard Shaw, Oscar Wilde and the novelist George Meredith, the society staged a private production of Shelley's verse drama *The Cenci*, with Kenneth in the role of Giacomo. A story of incest and murder – and banned since publication in 1819 by the Lord Chamberlain – *The Cenci* was strong meat for a Victorian audience. Predictable howls of outrage characterized the reviews that followed, including in the pages of the influential, eminently respectable *Pall Mall Gazette*. Furnivall's housemaid noticed Kenneth most of all, telling her employer, 'Mr Grahame did look so handsome walking up and down the stage in his best clothes.'[10] With no appetite for scandal – and no noticeable taste for theatricals – it was a commendation Kenneth would have gladly forgone. Escape to Tuscany allowed him to leave behind the possibility of notoriety by association. His impressions of Italy took no account of the volatile hot-bloodedness of *The Cenci*, the play's internecine sexual jealousy and murderous plotting. Such thoughts were anathema to Kenneth throughout his life. Sailors' Farewells were safely sentimental, charming in their aesthetic naivety, tokens of forgotten, vanished affection; the disturbing passions of Shelley's tragedy were altogether different. Instead his visit to the Villino Landau fixed an idea of 'the South' that Kenneth had first conceived in front of paintings by Filippo Lippo and Fra Angelico in the National Gallery, in the boisterous pungency of Italian restaurants in Soho, in tags of Virgil, Marcus Aurelius, Horace and Homer at St Edward's: sustaining, health-giving, restorative, inspiriting, but sexless withal. He wrote later that anything not the South was 'nothing' and that 'the mind may starve and pine in glacial surroundings'.[11]

He steeped himself in Florentine art and history. Local festivals gripped his imagination, this Scots exile of no fixed faith, schooled in the colourful rituals of Oxford Movement Anglicanism. He visited frescoes in nearby churches, absorbed by these rich devotional images as the Pinturicchio St Catherine had absorbed him in Trafalgar Square. With Annie he set off over the hills to Fiesole to see at close quarters a festival of the Virgin. A decade later, he reimagined the spectacle in a story. 'Carpets and gay-coloured stuffs were hung out of the windows, the church bells clamoured noisily, the little street was flower-strewn, and the whole population jostled each other along either side of it, chattering, shoving, and ordering each other to stand back.'[12] The day was one of bright May sunshine. Confusion between Annie and her mother about travel arrangements meant that she and Kenneth had to walk both ways. Their excursion lasted the whole day: they returned at seven o'clock in the evening. Annie's principal recollection was of Kenneth's storytelling. As they crossed the green hillsides, Annie remembered, Kenneth 'beguiled [the day] with delightful fairy tales', continuing a dialogue begun a decade earlier in Pitlochry. It does not suggest flirtation. Kenneth bought a souvenir, a majolica plaque of the Virgin and Child made by the Florentine firm of Cantagalli, in imitation of sixteenth-century originals by the della Robbia family. He hung it outside his next London home.

Shortly afterwards, Kenneth made a second visit to Italy, this time to Rome. In imagination he had often found himself in the city – this classically educated young man who had doodled in the margins of Macaulay's *Lays*, and later, to Helen's derision, declaimed their stately measure in the woods at Cranbourne. He found the reality a disappointment, and eventually would argue that, for a city of legend, it could not be otherwise. In Kenneth's essays Rome remains the 'Eternal City', the 'Golden City'. Many years later, under sadly altered circumstances, he returned. In 1890 his enjoyment of Venice – in his mind less hedged about by its own myths and storybook expectations – was more straightforward. He called it 'a fine city, wherein... the air is full of music and the sky full of stars, and the lights flash and shimmer on the polished steel prows of the swaying gondolas'.[13]

In the bank ledger he showed to Furnivall, Kenneth attempted to answer a question: 'Of the friends that make so great a part of our life, relentless Time makes two bodies – the living and the dead – which are the dearer?'[14] Kenneth chose the dead. 'Their sympathies are sure,' he wrote.

It was not the case in his own life, as he knew, though sweet Bessie Grahame was certainly an exception. At the end of February 1887, Cunningham Grahame died. He appears to have made no attempt to contact Kenneth – or Helen, Willie or Roland – in the twenty years following his departure for Normandy. The news arrived in the form of two telegrams sent by Uncle John Grahame's partner Mr Currie from the Le Havre office of Grahame, Spens and Currie. The first notified Kenneth of his father's stroke; the second, soon after, of his death, described as instantaneous.

Kenneth travelled to France overnight from Southampton. In his father's room, in a house belonging to an elderly Frenchwoman called Madame Bazille, Cunningham's tolerant and affectionate landlady for the last eighteen years, little remained to see bar the body: Currie had already cleared away any books and papers to the office. Kenneth's farewell was brief; the coffin was shortly closed. The burial took place the same afternoon. The resident Methodist minister, Mr Whelpton, conducted the service according to Anglican rites in the affordable cemetery at Sainte-Adresse to the north, 'on the heights overlooking the sea, near the lighthouses'. Kenneth's diary suggests a smallish knot of mourners: Madame Bazille, her son and daughter-in-law, Kenneth, Currie and clerks from Grahame, Spens and Currie. Afterwards, with Currie's approval, Kenneth gave Madame Bazille £5 – a sum rather greater then than now – and, still later, the fifteen francs he found in his father's pockets. To her son he gave his father's clothes. He declined Madame Bazille's offer in return of 'a small photo of [Cunningham] which he had given her, and which she wished me to take if I had not got one'.[15] Carefully he looked through the few possessions remaining in the rented room. From the office he selected books, including dictionaries: poor record of a life. He visited the docks, accompanied by a member of Currie's staff.

The following day, after consigning events to his diary in precise, unemotional prose, he returned to London. He never again referred directly to his father with any nearer approach to emotion. Kenneth's essay writing and subsequent fiction mostly bypass the question of parents; in his own life he pursued neither father nor mother substitutes, though Furnivall and his first editor W. E. Henley both fulfilled a quasi-paternal role as literary mentors. Instead, imprinted on virtually everything Kenneth wrote is the legacy of The Mount, that stretch of green English riverbank unknown to Cunningham Grahame, or the image of the Downs, where mostly Kenneth chose to walk alone.

In the second half of 1887, Frederick Greenwood, editor of the *St James's Gazette*, accepted Kenneth's essay 'By a Northern Furrow'. It was written in the shadow of Cunningham's death, a wintry meditation on the endless cycle of nature's renewal and, against this, the transitoriness of human life. On the subject of death, Kenneth quoted Tennyson and Walt Whitman; 'emblems of mortality' permeate his discussion of landscape and painting. His 'somewhat sad account of the past year's words and deeds' almost certainly had a private resonance.

He did not return to the theme. Greenwood accepted a second, quite different contribution, though he did not publish it until the autumn of 1890. In 'A Bohemian in Exile', Kenneth crafted the first of his tales of London men who flee the capital. Beyond the idea of abandonment, there are no obvious links to Cunningham. 'He doubtless chose wisely to enjoy life his own way, and to gather from the fleeting days what bliss they had to give, nor spend them in toiling for a harvest to be reaped when he was dust,' Kenneth concluded.[16] More than a verdict on his father's flight, it was a warning of time's evanescence aimed at city workers, himself among them. Even so cursory an inspection of Madame Bazille's spartan lodgings had revealed to him their stark absence of 'bliss'.

In the meantime Kenneth cast his net widely in pursuit of alternative outlets for his writing. To a handful of editors he despatched neat, hand-written essays, sometimes transcribed on Bank of England paper – his practice, as Reginald Inglis had seen, since at least 1882. On 18 September 1888, in response to one such, now lost, he received a letter from the editor of the *Cornhill Magazine*, a distinguished and widely read journal that had previously serialized novels by Eliot, Trollope and Hardy. 'Your little paper is too short and slight for the *Cornhill*,' James Payn wrote, 'but the humour it exhibits has struck me as being exceptional and leads me to hope that I may again hear from you.'[17] At a time when 'five out of six of my little meteorites came back to me', Kenneth remembered, Payn's response was sufficiently encouraging to merit keeping, although there is no evidence that he took up its invitation. His only surviving overtly humorous writing, 'Conversation between a Balcony and a Waterspout', a satire on the relationship of Irish Home Rule politician Charles Parnell and his mistress Katharine O'Shea, was published anonymously in November 1890 in the *St James's Gazette*.

Kenneth's determination remained dogged. He had not forgotten – and never would – John Grahame's refusal to fund a university education. 'The heroes of all history had always been noted for their unswerving constancy,' announces the child narrator of 'A Saga of the Seas'.[18] In Kenneth's own case, constancy was rewarded by a series of serendipitous literary encounters, beginning with Furnivall.

However, it was William Ernest Henley, in the decade after Kenneth met Furnivall, whose enthusiasm for Kenneth's writing transformed aspiration into reality. Ten years Kenneth's senior, belligerent but zealous, Henley had only one foot. (The other had been amputated as a result of tubercular arthritis in 1875.) A friend of Robert Louis Stevenson, he was the model for Long John Silver in *Treasure Island*, a novel that he had helped steer towards publication. Physical lameness did not diminish his pugilist's spirit. Opinionated, argumentative and energetic, he was a vociferous opponent of socialism, Puritanism and religious orthodoxies: art and empire made up his credo. In

January 1889 Henley was appointed editor of the Edinburgh weekly newspaper, the *Scots Observer*. The following year, in a bid to increase circulation, he rebranded the paper the *National Observer* and, in 1892, transferred operations from Scotland to London.

Henley accepted Kenneth's first offering, 'Of Smoking', while he himself was completing a monograph about Scottish portraitist Henry Raeburn; he published the essay in the *Scots Observer* in October 1890. Over the next four years, he printed twenty more of Kenneth's essays. He 'was the first Editor who gave me a full and a free and a frank show, who took all I had and asked me for more,' Kenneth remembered.[19] If Kenneth had not yet discovered for himself Stevenson's *Virginibus Puerisque*, a collection of essays published in 1881 and reissued in 1887, Henley certainly directed his attention towards it. *Virginibus Puerisque* is dedicated to Henley; an essay called 'Some Portraits by Raeburn' anticipates his own lengthier study. Kenneth's early essays for Henley closely retraced Stevenson's footprints. 'Loafing' echoes 'An Apology for Idlers', 'The Rural Pan' Stevenson's 'Pan's Pipes'. Stevenson had already articulated Kenneth's consistent underlying lament for the losses caused by the century's 'progress': 'Science writes of the world as if with the cold finger of a starfish; it is all true; but what is it when compared to the reality of which it discourses? where hearts beat high in April, and death strikes, and hills totter in the earthquake, and there is a glamour over all the objects of sight, and a thrill in all noises for the ear, and Romance herself has made a dwelling among men?'[20] Unsurprisingly, a critic labelled Kenneth's essays 'Stevensonettes'.

Henley's championing placed Kenneth within a stable of distinguished *National Observer* writers: W. B. Yeats, J. M. Barrie, Kipling, H. G. Wells. Henley also invested the business of writing with that camaraderie Kenneth shared with the more sympathetic of his Bank of England colleagues, including Sidney Ward, who accompanied him on walking weekends on the Downs, or the young men he worked alongside at Toynbee Hall and Whitechapel Art Gallery, among them the barrister with whom he later shared a house, Tom Greg. Caustic and vituperative on slender provocation, Henley was remarkable for his avuncular approach to nurturing talent. Yeats remembered him '[making] us feel always our importance, and no man among us could do good work, or show the promise of it, and lack his praise'; Stevenson referred to shared sympathy, 'founded on the love of our art, and nourished by mutual assistance'.[21] For favoured contributors, Henley hosted a weekly Friday-night supper at Solferino's in Rupert Street and Sunday 'at homes' in his house in Chiswick, 'in two rooms, with folding doors between, and hung... with photographs from Dutch masters, and in one room there was always... a table with cold meat'. Max Beerbohm's description of Henley's table at Solferino's as 'the Henley regatta' suggests a recognized group identity. Superficial or not, it gave Kenneth a sense of belonging. It legitimized his activities outside the bank.

At the outset, Kenneth benefited twice over from Henley's belief in him and Stevenson's absence. Henley's continuing admiration for the Stevenson-style essay, which Stevenson himself was unable to supply following his departure for America in 1887, left a void filled by Kenneth. In the first years of their association, *Virginibus Puerisque* provided Kenneth with a workable template for his contributions to Henley's paper. Like many young writers, Kenneth may have struggled to find material to sustain his eagerness to write. Henley's attachment to the 'Stevensonette' and its recognizably fin-de-siècle preoccupations – the thirst for oblivion, suspicion of modernity, personal bohemianism and nature mysticism – supplied Kenneth with a sympathetic agenda and saved him the problem of identifying appropriate subject matter. Kenneth's treatment of his subjects was his own: his love of landscape is frequently the dominant note. Avoiding overt didacticism, his touch is lighter than Stevenson's.

'Mr Henley supplied not only a haven for young writers, but also an impulse and momentum,' an anonymous critic claimed in 1897.[22] The price Henley exacted was an assertive, intrusive approach to his task of editing. Fond of classical allusions and archaic verbal flourishes, he embellished the work of all his contributors with his own bulky stylistic mannerisms. He was obdurate in the face of resistance: annotated proofs of an unpublished essay, 'A Funeral', reveal Henley's 'improvements' and Kenneth's protests. Only with publication of 'The Olympians', the first of Kenneth's non-Stevensonette stories about Edward, Selina, Charlotte and Harold, did his intervention lessen. Tactfully Kenneth would choose to remember his particular quality as vividness.

To at least one observer, Kenneth appeared at a gathering of 'the Henley regatta' in September 1891 'a tall, well-knit... man, who moved slowly and with dignity, and who preserved, amid the violent discussions and altercations that enlivened the meetings of the group, a calm, comprehending demeanour accompanied by a ready smile that women would call "sweet". And yet this... temperate, kindly-looking man had also a startled air, as a fawn might show who suddenly found himself on Boston Common...

unable to escape wholly from the memory of the glades and wood whence he had come. He seemed to be a man who had not yet become quite accustomed to the discovery that he was no longer a child... Every one of us has his adjective. His adjective was – startled.'[23]

Kenneth never would escape the memory of the glades and wood – the country round The Mount – and deliberately so. On these memories he built past, present and future happiness. To be 'as a fawn' – childlike – was both inadvertent and an aspiration, his protest against Olympians' barbarism and silliness. He praised the child's sense of wonder, 'the most priceless possession of the human race', and queried 'the use of living in a world devoid of wonderment'; in *The Wind in the Willows*, he eventually offered his riposte to an 'unwondering' world.[24] His Olympians stories are Wordsworthian, shaped by the poet's vision of the childish connection to the divine in the world around us, which Kenneth interpreted both as wonder and insight:

There was a time when meadow, grove and stream,
The earth, and every common sight,
To me did seem apparelled in celestial light,
The glory and the freshness of a dream.

'"There *was* a time",' Kenneth explained to an American

academic, quoting Wordsworth. 'It is *that* time which I have attempted to recapture and commemorate,' and not only in a handful of stories but in his conduct of his life.[25] Daily encounters did indeed startle him: his introduction to Frederick Fryer as a new boy at St Edward's, first exposure to his fellow clerks in the Bank of England – proof that his 'fourth dimension' offered only qualified protection. The habit of withdrawal within himself persisted. He lived his life in compartments. 'It is possible that he was somebody quite different in his official capacity at the Bank of England,' concluded Evelyn Sharp, who came across Kenneth at literary parties. He was childlike but not childish: stubbornly, he preserved his own version of the child's view.

Showcased in a series of essay-length stories in the 1890s, this distinctive outlook earned him the unqualified admiration of his contemporaries.

· 7 ·

'I liked to get my meals regular and
then to prop my back against a bit of
rock and snooze a bit, and wake up
and think of things going on'

IN THE PAGES of the *Scots Observer* Kenneth described himself as one of the 'labourers in the vineyard, toilers and swinkers, [for whom] the morning pipe is smoked in hurry and fear and a sense of alarums and excursions and fleeting trains'.[1]

There were shards of truth in his affable narrative posturing. By 1890, Kenneth had been at the Bank of England for more than a decade. Soon Henley would begin pressing him to resign, to concentrate instead on writing full time, but Kenneth either did not intend, or was insufficiently brave, to leave yet. A transfer to the chief cashier's office in 1888 had been followed a year later by a second move, to the secretary's office; in the directors' library he catalogued books, 'mainly on dry-as-dust subjects'.[2] Bank of England routine was less exacting than that of many workplaces, its toil less toilsome: it imposed constraints nonetheless. In Chelsea Gardens, where work could be set aside, Kenneth forced himself to the 'pleasurable agony of attempting stately sentences of English prose'.[3] The 'toil [of] making sentences', he reflected, meant 'sitt[ing] indoors for many hours, cramped above a desk', while across the river in Battersea Park lay the distracting possibility that the wind was 'singing in the willows'.[4]

In the secretary's office, Kenneth worked alongside Sidney Ward, also a co-worker at Toynbee Hall. The men became friends, Sidney nearer to Kenneth in character than clerks of the spitting, dog-fighting, sheep-butchering, drunken variety: he recognized Kenneth's self-containment. Kenneth, he knew, 'liked a solitary life as a bachelor, with his books and writing, so that, friends as we were, I never saw a great deal of him outside our office life'. Correctly he estimated that 'he was probably the better pleased to see me because I didn't dig him out too often'.[5]

At Kenneth's invitation Sidney shared walking weekends in the Berkshire Downs and Chilterns. Sidney's account of one of these weekends suggests the bachelor chumminess of Jerome K. Jerome's *Three Men in a Boat*, published in the same year. One cold, sunny spring weekend, a friend lent Kenneth a fourteenth-century cottage on the tree-studded main street of Streatley, 'and we had a grand twenty-mile walk along the Ridgeway... If we either of us said clever things that day they are forgotten, but we came home happy and tired, bought some chops and fetched a huge jug of beer from the pub. We cooked our dinner over the open wood fire, and how good the chops were! Then great chunks of cheese, new bread, great swills of beer, pipes, bed, and heavenly sleep!'[6] Kenneth matched Sidney's enjoyment: nearly twenty years later, he revisited their weekends in the peaceable male companionship of *The Wind in the Willows*. 'Mole and Rat kicked the fire up, drew their chairs in, brewed themselves a last nightcap of mulled ale, and discussed the events of the long day. At last the Rat, with a tremendous yawn... clambered into his bunk and rolled himself well up in the blankets, and slumber gathered him forthwith, as a swath of barley is folded into the arms of the reaping-machine.'[7]

In the second half of 1894, Kenneth was appointed acting secretary of the Bank of England. Four years later, at the young age of thirty-nine, this appointment was confirmed. As secretary he occupied one of the bank's three senior positions; among more congenial tasks was the presidency of the bank's Library and Literary Association.[8] There is no reason to assume that promotion altered his view of City life, or the bank's activities in particular. A family friend criticized an attitude on Kenneth's part, decried as half-heartedness; as late as 1895, Kenneth revealed the extent of his ambivalence in a description of a nightmarish vision of a City clerk stalked on the Underground by the 'old – oh, so very old' figure of Death.[9] In 'The Headswoman', the youthful executioner, Jeanne, summarizes her role as 'an occupation demanding punctuality, concentration, judgement, – all the qualities, in fine, that go to make a good business man', a statement that tells us something of Kenneth's thoughts concerning commerce and finance. For good measure, she dismisses the law, that other refuge of Grahame men, as 'a minor and less exacting walk of life' than her own line in corporal punishment.

Kenneth's version of the Streatley weekend in 'The Romance of the Road' suggests that he endured the week-day world by cultivating forgetfulness. It points to the persistence of other aspirations, too. 'After unnumbered chops with country ale, the hard facts of life begin to swim in a golden mist. You are isled from accustomed cares and worries... old failures seem partial successes... Tomorrow you shall begin life again: shall write your book, make your fortune, do anything; meanwhile you sit.'[10] Although this is unlikely to represent the whole truth, the inference is clear: oblivion induced by physical exertion and over-indulgence offered respite from regretfulness, made the Bank of England tolerable. Kenneth's contentment appears less than that of Mole and Rat, whose lives are entirely leisured. As a guarantee of happiness, his childhood habit of oscillating between actual and imaginary worlds yielded variable success in the face of the bank's solid realities. To himself, Kenneth admitted that he was not one of the 'stout-hearted ones' who have 'the rare courage, at the realizing point, to kick the board over and declare against further play'.[11] This much had been clear as early as 1879 and his arrival at the bank in line with John Grahame's contriving. His rebellion was always submerged; his desire to 'kick the board over' was at best intermittent.

'The Romance of the Road' appeared in the *National Observer* in February 1891. That autumn, Henley published a story by Kenneth written in the first person, apparently from a child's point of view. 'The Olympians' is about adults and children and the gulf between them, the imbalance of power in adults' favour, their unthinking social conformity. The narrative voice belongs at once to the child and his grown-up self. The influence of Stevenson hovers, in this case an essay called 'Child's Play' in which, through a child's eyes, adults appear 'bearded or petticoated giants... who move upon a cloudy Olympus'.[12] After an interval of eighteen months, Kenneth wrote five more stories, using the same unidentified child narrator. Only Harold appears alongside him in 'The Olympians'. In 'A Whitewashed Uncle', 'The Finding of the Princess', 'Young Adam Cupid', 'The Burglars' and 'Snowbound', completed between February and September 1893, the reader is introduced to Edward, Selina and Charlotte, as well as Aunt Eliza, sundry uncles and Miss Smedley the governess. The condition of the five parentless children, 'whose nearest were aunts and uncles', mirrors that of the Grahame children. The three boys reflect aspects of Kenneth himself: Edward his talent for bluff conformity,

Harold his giddy imagination, the narrator's preference for his own company. They live at The Mount, sketchily outlined save for the lingering details of garden and surrounding country.

The genesis of these stories is unclear. On 19 January 1893, Kenneth wrote to John Lane of the publishing house The Bodley Head. To date, Henley had published twenty contributions by Kenneth in the *National Observer*, including three poems and 'The Olympians'. At Henley's prompting, he offered Lane a selection of pieces for compilation in book form, in the manner of *Virginibus Puerisque*. With a mixture of diffidence and defiance, he wrote, 'Mr Henley suggested to me once, that a "blend" of these short articles with verse would perhaps make a "feature" that might take. But that is a detail I have no particular feeling about, one way or the other.'[13] He added, 'They are, I think, just sufficiently individual and original to stand it.'

In individuality, 'The Olympians' clearly outstripped Kenneth's 'Stevensonettes'. Its charming, funny, bittersweet presentation of childish percipience was little less than radical to a late-Victorian readership conditioned to objectify children sentimentally. Whether it was Kenneth himself who acknowledged this or Lane or Henley or all three is unclear. At least one contemporary accorded the laurels to Henley. 'It may be that when the history of the *Scots* and *National Observer* is written... we shall then know whether... it was [Mr Grahame's] own idea to continue the diverting narrative of the childhood of Harold and Edward, Charlotte and Selina,' ran an unsigned article in the *Academy* in December 1897. 'As the cause of wit in others Mr Henley holds a very high position.'[14] Whichever way, for a writer who would always work slowly, the result was the equivalent of creative frenzy. John Lane included all six stories – and no poems – in his selection.

The agreement Kenneth negotiated with Lane was impressive. 'I don't call this a grasping proposal – especially from a Scotchman,' he wrote, presumably disingenuously.[15] Lane – notoriously slippery about money – almost certainly disagreed. Heredity, fourteen years at the bank or even Uncle John Grahame may have stiffened Kenneth's hand. On a short publishing run of 450 copies, he stipulated royalties of 10 per cent on the first 200 sold, rising to 20 per cent thereafter. Surprisingly Lane acquiesced. He published the collection in October 1893 under the title *Pagan Papers*, with a voguish black-and-white illustration by Aubrey Beardsley on the title page. For the first time Kenneth enjoyed the sight of his name attached to work that had first appeared anonymously.

Reviews were mixed. Correctly, critics identified the book's derivative qualities; the more conservative press jibbed at the idea of paganism. Paganism was a buzzword of the moment, an umbrella term, shorthand for a strand of anti-authoritarianism. It targeted key Victorian orthodoxies of religion, culture and morality; it was invariably nostalgic. The figure of Pan – half-man, half-god – became a key symbol: vigorous, untrammelled in his natural urges, protesting, piliferous, priapic.

Measured against these generalizations, *Pagan Papers* is 'pagan' only in its dislike of modernity and an intense engagement with nature. Kenneth claimed that the part of his brain he used in early childhood had never altered. His perceptions, he was convinced, were those of a child, and it was children, he believed, who preserved links with the natural world that adults routinely severed. In his weekend persona, combing the hills and fields, he insisted on his own physical and emotional connectedness to the landscape. His view of nature was egalitarian: he assumed equality between himself and the creatures of field and hedge and wood. (Later, in an essay called 'The Inner Ear', he would go a step further and claim that, while man needed nature, the dependency was not mutual: 'it is evident that we are entirely superfluous'.) His 'paganism' was pastoralism, a cult of the country, a facet of his social and political conservatism; he banished the glum Scots Protestantism of Mrs Inglis and Uncle John Grahame in favour of a mysticism centred on nature. Kenneth's Pan is a nature spirit, a symbol of the older, vanishing, pre-industrialized landscape to which Kenneth was so fiercely attached: like Kenneth, he is wary of the jangling vulgarities of the age, its materialism, the helter-skelter pursuit of novelty. In 'The Rural Pan', Pan 'loveth the more unpretentious humankind, especially them that are... addicted to the kindly soil, and to the working thereof: perfect in no way, only simple, cheery sinners'.[16] With no interest in acknowledging sexual urges of his own, Kenneth also stripped his Pan of lechery. The result is a poster boy for his own rural nostalgia – as he understood, a minority viewpoint. Kenneth's Pan endorses all the author's hobbyhorses, as will Rat, Mole and Badger in *The Wind in the Willows*: his paganism is imaginative escapism.[17] It was shaped by the games he had played in the garden at The Mount, and children's books read in boyhood and since. It was decorative, even whimsical. 'A step into the woodland was a step over the margin... and then, good-bye to the modern world,' he wrote in 'Deus Terminus', included in *Pagan Papers*. 'Little hands were stretched to trip you, fairy gibe and mockery pelted you from every rabbit-hole.' In its emphasis on long walks and country pubs, his paganism was hearty, too. He lamented his contemporaries' resistance to 'jigs and fantasies'.[18]

Kenneth had good reason for his lasting gratitude to Henley. Enthusiastically, Henley had welcomed him into his stable of contributors. He had encouraged him to pursue publication of his 'Stevensonettes' in book form. His recommendation had gone some way to persuading John Lane of an uncertain venture. In bringing about Kenneth's association with Lane, Henley placed his protégé in the way of another key introduction – to an erratic, excitable, shrilly spoken, short-sighted, long-haired ex-pat American novelist and short story writer, 'an incalculable creature of moods, at one moment sneering and unjust and the next serious and appreciative': Henry Harland.[19]

Although accounts conflict, Harland appears to have conceived the idea of a new kind of periodical, in which artwork and literary contributions were independent of one another but accorded equal status, in the summer of 1893. He would edit it himself, with Aubrey Beardsley as art editor; it would have 'the courage of its modernity and not tremble at the frown of Mrs Grundy'. His coup was to secure John Lane as his publisher. Lane agreed to issue the periodical quarterly, bound in yellow wrappers, like illicit French novels of the period. Max Beerbohm offered a fictionalized account of key decisions in a sketch set in the autumn of 1893, in which Beardsley tells him, 'Most exciting! John Lane wants to bring out a Quarterly – Writings and Drawings – Henry Harland to be Literary Editor – Me to be Art Editor. Great fun... Not just a *paper* thing. A *bound* thing: a real *book*, bound in good thick boards. *Yellow* ones. Bright yellow, and it's going to be called *The Yellow Book*.'[20] The plan was unveiled at an evening of heavy drinking at London's Devonshire Club in February 1894, two months ahead of the first issue.

Publication of *Pagan Papers* went some way to establishing a literary reputation for Kenneth. In its aftermath, Henley printed six more 'Olympians' stories as well as three new 'Stevensonettes' over the course of ten months. For the *National Observer*, however, time was running out. The paper had consistently lost money. In the late summer of 1894 it closed. Kenneth's final contribution was the witty, risqué 'Sawdust and Sin', in which Charlotte tells a version of *Alice in Wonderland* to two of her dolls, Rosa and Jerry, and the dolls' inability to sit up without slumping against one another is presented as an attempted seduction of blonde Rosa by black-haired Jerry. The loss of Henley's paper inevitably jeopardized the prospects of any new Olympians stories.

The Yellow Book came to Kenneth's rescue. Harland first approached him, at John Lane's prompting, in the spring of 1894. By then Kenneth not only understood the parlousness of affairs at the *National Observer*, but his yardstick for literary success had altered dramatically. In April, his cousin Anthony Hope Hawkins gave up his practice at the Bar. Four years earlier he had paid for publication of a novel, *A Man of Mark*, that failed to attract attention. With *The Prisoner of Zenda*, written under the pseudonym Anthony Hope, he found himself an overnight sensation and retired to write full time. Such conspicuous success when Kenneth's own literary future was tottering unsettled his more cautious cousin.

The same month, a storm of protest greeted the first *Yellow Book*. It was not the fault of blameless contributions by Frederic Leighton, Walter Crane and Edmund Gosse (afterwards librarian to the House of Lords). Outrage targeted an essay by Max Beerbohm in praise of cosmetics, including 'sun tan' makeup for men, and Arthur Symons's poem, 'Stella Maris', about an encounter with a prostitute ('The chance romances of the streets,/... One night we loved each other well'), in which Symons praised his 'Juliet of a night' in terms more often associated with the Virgin Mary. Moral opprobrium, once earned, proved lasting. Throughout its three-year lifespan, *The Yellow Book* was synonymous with subversion: effete, libertine, decadent.

It seems a surprising forum for Kenneth's poignantly

humorous stories about children, and for a writer of his stamp. Kenneth's satire against 'the Olympians' targeted their lack of imagination. He protested against unthinking convention, not conformity, like the Dragon in 'The Reluctant Dragon' who complains about fighting St George: 'the whole thing's nonsense and conventionality and popular thick-headedness'.[21] Amiable and upright, Kenneth had no interest in shocking, as he had demonstrated in his retreat to Tuscany amid the brouhaha following Furnivall's production of *The Cenci*; he had little in common with *Yellow Book* contributors like the troubled poet Lionel Johnson – a repressed homosexual alcoholic Catholic convert – or Johnson's fellow poet, the foppish Richard Le Gallienne. His outlook was closer to Lane's. Both identified in Harland's venture sound commercial opportunities and, in Kenneth's case, a continuing readership. *The Yellow Book*'s ambitions were lofty. Critically acclaimed and advanced in their presentation of children, Kenneth's stories satisfied its remit of courageous modernity. His first contribution, published in July, was 'The Roman Road', among the very best of his Olympians stories.

His participation in the social world gathered around Harland and his wife Aline was less comfortable than his membership of Henley's 'regatta'. He regularly attended the Harlands' Saturday evenings in the Cromwell Road; he 'always seem[ed] to want to get into a corner and evade notice if possible'.[22] With Henry, Aline and Evelyn Sharp – then a writer of fairy tales for *The Yellow Book* – he spent Christmas 1895 in Brussels and, the following winter, travelled to Boulogne. Otherwise he had little in common with Harland's troubled young men, as women in the group were quick to discern. One noted Kenneth's 'complete freedom from the affectations which so puzzled me in the other men of the set': 'He answered my idea of a *man* and I suppose half-consciously... I was comparing him with the more or less effeminate young men I met there.'[23] He reminded Evelyn Sharp 'of the nicest kind of schoolboy except that he had a fine taste in literature instead of a passion for sport. He had a charming sense of humour and was a great tease.'[24] For Sharp, he was 'very kind and courteous [with] not an ounce of humbug in him'. Tellingly, short story writer Netta Syrett concluded that 'he was sane and normal'. All three women contrasted Kenneth positively with the run of *Yellow Book* men.

In the event, Kenneth was not so 'sane and normal' as to guard against an occurrence that could have been lifted from one of his 'Stevensonettes' about fugitive City men. After a heavy evening with the Harlands, he staggered as far as Piccadilly, where he saw a vegetable

cart heading towards Covent Garden. Kenneth gave chase
and climbed aboard. On his bed of cabbages, 'overcome by
an "exposition of sleep"', he promptly passed out.[25] The
costermonger looked kindly on his drunken passenger
dressed in evening clothes. When Kenneth woke up in the
early hours, he was retracing his steps to Piccadilly, still in
the cart, which was now empty of vegetables. Later, he was
sorry, he told a friend, 'that he never knew what happened
in the interval'.

Like Henley before him, Harland nurtured Kenneth's
writing. The immediate result was completion of 'The
Headswoman', his historical fantasy begun in 1890, before
'The Olympians' changed the direction of his fiction
writing. Published in *The Yellow Book* in October, it is a
story influenced by aspects of Kenneth's working life,
and the bulk of its satire is directed against officialdom.
In spirit, seventeenth-century Jeanne is a New Woman
of the 1890s: her protest is a plea for women's rights. The
pleasure of decapitation by so attractive and engaging an
executioner provides the story's central joke – literally,
gallows humour. Evelyn Sharp, who would become a
prominent suffragist, clearly preferred Kenneth's Olympians stories, also the verdict of subsequent readers.
'The appearance of one of his sketches in the YB would
be hailed as an event and discussed at length the next

Saturday evening,' she remembered. She does not mention 'The Headswoman', which John Lane nevertheless issued in stand-alone form the following year.[26]

Only two more Olympians stories were published in *The Yellow Book*. Instead Kenneth offered new stories to Henley, who was back on his feet as editor of the *New Review*: published monthly, the *New Review* offered more opportunities than Harland's quarterly. Additional stories were also published in American journals *The Chapbook* and *Scribner's Magazine*. Kenneth and John Lane were equally enthusiastic about a second compilation on the lines of *Pagan Papers*. In *The Golden Age*, published in February 1895, were twelve new Olympians stories and no 'Stevensonettes'; Lane also included the six stories already published in *Pagan Papers*. The result was an instant success, crowned by an effusive review by poet Algernon Swinburne, who described the book as 'well nigh too praiseworthy for praise', royalty payments, invitations from society hostesses, inclusion as one of only two English-language books on the bookshelf of Kaiser Wilhelm's cabin in his royal yacht, the *Hohenzollern*, alongside the Bible. In vain dissenting voices challenged Kenneth's destruction of the myth of the innocent, ignorant Beautiful Child: Lane's first reprint appeared in March. Within a year Kenneth had matched the achievement of his cousin Anthony

Hope Hawkins. Unlike Hope Hawkins, he did not resign his day job.

By the spring of 1895, Kenneth had succeeded in the career Uncle John Grahame had forced upon him; he had also succeeded in his own ambition to become a writer. From childhood he had lived two lives. During the 1890s, he rationalized those two lives as a series of polarities: 'toiler' and idler; senior administrator and loafer; Grahame probity versus artistic fulfilment; active and passive. This conflict was self-generated and self-serving; it inspired him creatively.

In 'The Reluctant Dragon', written in 1898, he created a trio of fictional self-portraits: a bookish young boy, St George and a dragon. Both dragon and saint unwillingly undertake the parts allotted to them by traditional narratives. Neither has any appetite for their preordained roles or their inevitable showdown. Chivvied by the boy, they agree to a public contest; as in the storybooks, St George emerges apparently victorious. The sonnet-writing Dragon comes closest to Kenneth's personal mythmaking: 'so engaging and so trustful, and as simple as a child'.[27] 'All the other fellows were so active and *earnest* and all that sort of thing,' he tells the Boy, describing other dragons, 'always rampaging, and skirmishing, and scouring the desert sands, and pacing the margin of the sea, and chasing knights all over the place, and devouring damsels, and going on generally – whereas I liked to get my meals regular and then to prop my back against a bit of rock and snooze a bit, and wake up and think of things going on and how they kept going on just the same'.[28]

Kenneth, of course, was both kinds of dragon. His weekends on the Downs involved scouring and pacing aplenty to satisfy his active side: his requirement for 'meals regular' and things 'going on just the same' were assumptions of the banker secure in his purse and content with the status quo. Absent from Threadneedle Street, Kenneth propped his back against a bit of rock and daydreamed and reimagined his daydreams as fiction: the dragon who, in place of action, exasperates the boy with 'views and theories of life and personal tendencies, and all that sort of thing'.[29]

Like the dragon, celebrated, successful, lionized Kenneth would meet his own St George. She appeared in surprising guise and at a moment of defencelessness to lure him unexpectedly to his defeat.

· 8 ·

'Woman as but a drab thing'

'Hitherto we had known the outward woman as but a drab thing, hour-glass shaped, nearly leg-less, bunched here, constricted there; slow of movement,' Kenneth wrote in 1896.[1] The statement belongs to the adult writer, at the age of thirty-seven, as much as to the childish narrator to whom he attributes it. It follows an ecstatic description of a circus performer called Coralie. She is dressed in 'pink and spangles'. Her white arms are bare; her legs are visible. She is golden-haired and her beauty strikes Kenneth's narrator as 'more than mortal'. Fleetingly, he is in love.

Love had scarcely touched Kenneth himself. Bessie Grahame brimmed over with maternal love, but died much too soon to draw her children's emotional horizons or even leave behind her any residue of unconditional affection; their father's preoccupations were directed inwards. Neither Mrs Inglis nor Uncle John Grahame had rated emotional wellbeing uppermost in their duty of care to Cunningham's orphans. The standard brutalities of nineteenth-century boarding school, added to the shock of Willie's death, further dammed any overflow of feel-ings in Kenneth and Roland. Helen's brusqueness masked strong sibling affection. John Grahame had insisted that Kenneth participate in the adult, masculine world of work, away from Cranbourne and brother and sister, within months of his sixteenth birthday. Unsurprisingly, Kenneth's childhood daydreaming had hardened into a preference, amounting to a requirement, for solitude: only solitude, he believed, let the mind shake off its harness, thoughts be liberated, creativity stimulated, 'for, be he who may, if there is another fellow present, your mind has to trot between shafts'.[2] In their first years at the Bank of England, with reservations on Kenneth's part, he and Roland had lived together briefly in Bloomsbury Street. In 1882 Kenneth made the break, choosing to live alone.

He gave up the Chelsea flat after a dozen years to set up house at 5 Kensington Crescent with Tom Greg, an amiable barrister 'of rugged vitality and ever-present sympathy', whom he had met at Toynbee Hall. Kenneth's reasons for this change are unclear, but as acting secretary of the bank he may have been required to entertain at home on a larger, more formal scale; Annie Grahame believed he had tired of looking after himself and craved the services of a live-in cook-housekeeper who could not be accommodated in a flat. Tom Greg shared Kenneth's sideline in journalism, a series of essays on wine published in the *Pall Mall Gazette* and the *National Observer*; he contributed to the *Art Journal*, the *Manchester Guardian*, the *Birmingham Daily Post*. Of a wealthy mill-owning family from Cheshire, he collected early English and continental pottery, later loaning ceramics described as 'pre-Wedgwood' to a museum in Manchester; his tastes influenced Kenneth's. His library included a two-volume first edition of Grimm's fairy tales in handsome Morocco bindings. Epicureanism supplied a further link. In *The Wind in the Willows*, Rat defines his world as 'brother and sister... and aunts, and company, and food and drink, and (naturally) washing'.[3] Kenneth could have said something similar, with food and drink not least on the list – like Rat's breathless picnic menu of 'coldtonguecoldhamcoldbeefpickledgherkinssaladfrench-rollscresssandwichespottedmeatgingerbeerlemonadesoda-water' or the picture of his own pantry Kenneth drew in a story called 'Bertie's Escapade': 'cold chicken, tongue, pressed beef, jellies, trifle *and* champagne', 'apples, oranges, chocolates, ginger and crackers'.[4]

The men employed a housekeeper, Sarah Bath: an out-spoken woman of black-and-white convictions, low church bias and decided outlook, from Somerset. Jointly they oversaw a generous table and a full cellar. 'With port we lose the senses, with claret we exchange them,' Greg wrote; he considered port the prince of wines, and, 'across the dinner table, in smoking-room armchairs', Kenneth's evenings at home were full of like-minded conviviality.[5] Anecdotal evidence paints Sarah Bath as a battleaxe. She told Kenneth that she mistrusted writers, whom she considered 'loose fish'. She preferred bankers – as Kenneth pointed out to her, by the same analogy, 'goldfish'. She prided herself on a job well done and provided for her bachelor charges high levels of comfort. Kenneth affixed to the outside of the house the Cantagalli plaque of the Madonna and Child he had bought with Annie Grahame in Florence. A visiting cousin noted his irritation at Greg's particular taste in pictures and manner of hanging them. For the most part the arrangement was a happy one.

It lasted a year. In 1895 Tom Greg became engaged to Mary Hope, leaving Kenneth in Kensington Crescent, in Sarah Bath's capable care, with a new housemate, Gregory Smith. Kenneth's reaction to this unexpectedly sudden departure has not survived: in itself it was not enough to point his thoughts inevitably towards marriage. 1895 found him particularly busy. Outside the bank he was occupied by the success of *The Golden Age* and engaged on a series of new stories that would make up its sequel; Henley published two new pieces in the *New Review* in March and a third in October. Like every *Yellow Book* contributor, he was concerned by the trial of Oscar Wilde. At the point of arrest on 5 April, Wilde was carrying a French novel: with its bright covers, journalists mistook it for *The Yellow Book*. Reaction to Wilde's 'crimes' was virulent. It did not spare *The Yellow Book* and the journal's offices at

The Bodley Head were stoned. 'Uncleanliness is next to Bodliness,' *Punch* quipped, to Kenneth's horror. A decade ago, he had removed himself physically from the backlash that followed performance of *The Cenci*. On this occasion, troubled by *Punch*'s insinuation, he suggested that Lane sue, and further detached himself from 'Wildean' elements of Harland's journal. 'I do not care for notoriety: in fact it is distasteful to me,' he commented later.[6] Save the story to which he was already committed, 'Dies Irae', Kenneth published only one new piece in *The Yellow Book* after Wilde's arrest. 'To Rollo, Untimely Taken' was a poem on the death of a puppy. While it did little to enhance Kenneth's literary reputation, its simple sentiment and clumsy classical name-checks were comfortably remote from the 'decadent' aestheticism vilified by the journal's detractors.

Kenneth's avoidance of marriage hitherto was just one outcome of his determination to preserve a childlike outlook that, on the cusp of middle age, held firm. A guest at a lunch party in 1896, admiring *The Golden Age*, admitted her anxiety that the author would grow up and be prevented from writing new stories. Kenneth had recently completed 'The Magic Ring', about a visit to a circus, in which the narrator's pulse is quickened by white-limbed Coralie and a dusky equestrienne called Zephyrine. To his fellow guest his reassurance was quick: 'No – I don't think I shall – I've just been writing about a circus and I found I didn't feel a bit grown up,' he told her.[7] Descriptions of both circus women tell a different story. Zephyrine, 'the Bride of the Desert', is a 'magnificent, full-figured Cleopatra'. Her exoticism is tangibly erotic. The grown-up longings uncovered belong to Kenneth rather than his childish narrator.

Fear as much as anything shaped his stubbornness about growing up. Death, abandonment and upheaval had effectively destroyed his childhood. Stunned and uncomprehending, as a young child he had created for himself a substitute world in his imagination. In the short years at The Mount, he invented and enjoyed a private golden age. Afterwards he retained an overwhelming attachment to it. The loose sequence of stories that was not yet complete preserved key memories of the feverish joy he had contrived after the loss of both his parents and in defiance of Mrs Inglis and Uncle John Grahame. Despite outward success in his thirties, these fantasies of early childhood remained the clearest instance of autonomy in Kenneth's life. They represented something more, too. The period of intense, selective memory from the ages of five to seven was the only interval in his life when imagination at its most powerful combined with a child's limited emotional understanding to overcome every faculty of reason and successfully smother misery: he simply imagined so hard that nothing else felt real. For Kenneth the act of writing his fact-and-fiction Olympians stories resuscitated former happiness, with its astonishing anaesthetizing of despair. In resisting growing up, Kenneth showed himself unwilling to discard childish escapism and confront unhappiness that, as a child, he had sidelined.

He was also poorly equipped for loving relationships. Since his departure from Cranbourne for St Edward's, his world had been as strenuously male as 'the succession of books on sport, in which the illustrator seemed to have forgotten that there were such things as women in the world' against which Selina protests in a story called 'Its Walls were as of Jasper'.[8] Although women were admitted to the clerical staff of the Bank of England in 1890 and *The Yellow Book* had its share of female contributors, Kenneth mostly worked among men; men made up his fellow volunteers in the London Scottish, at Toynbee Hall and on the committee of the New Shakspere Society. Kenneth's life was well ordered: it suited him. A development as fundamental as marriage would require wholesale readjustment. 'For myself, I rather liked a fair amount of blood-letting, red-hot shot, and flying splinters, but when you have girls about the place, they have got to be considered to a certain extent,' explains the narrator of one of the last Olympians stories.[9]

In his writing, there are signs that Kenneth's thoughts were edging inconclusively towards marriage some time before he committed himself. Both his writing and his correspondence indicate that this shift was accompanied by persistent misgivings. In her autobiography, Evelyn Sharp, who twice accompanied Kenneth and the Harlands abroad for Christmas, recorded that Henry Harland was eager to promote an attachment between them. Her memories of Kenneth after his death indicate that she may not have been averse to this; acerbic novelist Baron Corvo remembered her 'huge black eyes [that] yearned for the secretary of a bank'.[10] They saw one another regularly at *Yellow Book* gatherings in Cromwell Road and shared the same enjoyment of fairy tales that had previously linked Kenneth to Annie Grahame. Evelyn wrote to him frequently, usually with invitations. As often, he declined. References to books and stories pepper their notes. One letter suggests his impatience; he appears frightened of an escalating involvement. He accused Evelyn of rushing him in a manner he labelled 'hysterical'. He told her she reminded him 'of a Spanish bull-fight somehow – a flash of white horns, hot muzzles, a streak of red, a jump, a shout, – & all under a glittering Southern sun – or a St Moritz toboggin[sic] run', and held her firmly at arm's length.[11] Devastatingly for Evelyn, a markedly naïve, sensitive young woman of willowy appearance, he likened her to a Bandersnatch, a ferocious long-necked adversary in Lewis Carroll's *Jabberwocky* and *The Hunting of the Snark*, a comparison from which she could wring no dreg of affection. In this instance it is Kenneth, not Evelyn, who appears hysterical. His letter recalls the fear and loathing of a 'Stevensonette' called 'The Fairy Wicket', published in 1892, in which female attractiveness is presented as a trap and 'the depth of one sole pair of eyes' does not admit the loving swain to fairyland, but lures him through the gate of 'a cheap suburban villa, banging behind the wrathful rate-collector or hurled open to speed the pallid householder to the Registrar's Office'.[12] No wonder Evelyn remembered a look about Kenneth 'as if he thought you might be going to bite if he wasn't very careful'.[13]

Young boys' interest in the opposite sex permeates *The Golden Age*. In the last stories Kenneth wrote, published in book form as *Dream Days* in December 1898, this curiosity is intensified, as if the writer's own preoccupation had sharpened. The narrator reveals a secret to a girl who has caught his eye in church, in 'Mutabile Semper'. Rapidly he regrets the revelation. Such is his thraldom that, setting doubt aside, he agrees to meet her again. He keeps the date, but she spurns him for the ferret-owning son of a local clergyman. In 'Its Walls were as of Jasper', absorbed in a picture book, the narrator is curious about the truth of adult relationships: 'they were going to live happily ever after; and *that* was the part I wanted to get to. Story-books were so stupid, always stopping at the point where they became really nice.'[14] The book that he has counted on to supply this knowledge is briskly snatched from him. In both instances the narrator is disappointed. Significantly his regret is brief. Having been thrown over by the girl, he becomes 'aware of a certain solace and consolation in my newly recovered independence of action'.[15] Without the book, he reveals that what really interested him were not details of the couple's future but a picture of an island that has gripped his imagination. He longs to be transported to it and reassures himself that 'somehow, at some time, sooner or later, I was destined to arrive'.[16] He carries seeds of his preferred form of happiness within himself, 'self-poised', as an admirer referred to Kenneth.[17] Both stories toy with the idea of emotion; both revert to escapist fantasies. Neither can have made encouraging reading for any young woman who had set the stories' author in her sights.

Frank Dicksee's portrait of the nineteen-year-old Elspeth Thomson, painted in 1881, depicts her as a fashionable heroine. Hers is not mainstream fashion. The self-possessed young woman with the long, oval face and enormous doe eyes of challenging fixedness wears an amethyst brocade dress and a gold necklace of coloured stones: opals, garnets, tiny green cabochons. Hers is 'artistic' dress, her tastes advanced – and the painting was exhibited the year after at the Grosvenor Gallery, spiritual home of the pre-Raphaelites. Her clothes align her with the fashionable intelligentsia; her portrait is as much manifesto as likeness. The artistic pretensions it trumpets accurately reflect her aspirations, as does an expression of steely, unflinching determination that belies initial sweetness. This whimsical gazelle of a girl, pictured against a sludgy, 'greenery-yallery' backdrop of dim foliage and flowers, was a force to be reckoned with.

In 1897, when she first met the celebrated writer Kenneth Grahame, Elspeth Thomson was midway between thirty and forty, an unnerving age for a woman in a society that validated marriage as her only purpose; her appearance was still girlish. Her surface sophistication matched his urbanitas. His practised courtesy and charming witticisms found an echo in her easy knowledge of the worlds of art, letters and politics. As a child she had charmed Mark Twain, Alfred Tennyson, illustrator of the *Alice* books John Tenniel, who continued to send her Valentine's Day verses; like Kenneth, she had no intention of relinquishing her childhood self. Both Kenneth Grahame and Elspeth Thomson were adults in thrall to their childhoods: in Kenneth's case because childish escape consistently made him happy; in Elspeth's because growing up had brought her disappointments – her girlish charm insufficient to win her a husband, her friendship with literary giants not enough to make her a literary talent. Both were also children masquerading as adults: desperately naïve and emotionally unfulfilled; sexual novices. On the subject of sexual inexperience Kenneth described himself as hindered by 'much natral "gaucherie" wot as never been strove gainst'; he referred to 'my beastly virtue [that] has been my enemy through life'.[18] It was true of both of them. They recognized shared qualities in one another. Biographers accuse Elspeth Thomson of pouncing on Kenneth as her last chance of marriage.

The year that they met, Kenneth had been forced to re-evaluation. Roland Grahame married a young widow with two sons, Joan Fieling. Kenneth knew Joan, too: her son Tony wrote the original 'death letter' that he incorporated in 'Mutabile Semper' as Harold's riposte to Selina. Roland's marriage came as a jolt; Kenneth joined his brother and new sister-in-law for their first Christmas together. It was the first time a fully physical relationship between a man and woman had intruded upon the Grahames' immediate family circle.

Whatever the direction of his thoughts, Kenneth's meeting with Elspeth was an accident, probably a result of a visit to her stepfather, John Fletcher Moulton, on bank business at home in Onslow Square. In Fletcher Moulton's absence, Kenneth was entertained by Elspeth. Since her mother's death in 1888, she had kept house for the barrister and former MP; she was his hostess and occasional, unofficial secretary. Early on she and Kenneth identified similarities in upbringing: both born in Edinburgh (Elspeth's father Robert Thomson, who died in 1873, was the gifted entrepreneurial inventor of pneumatic tyres and a floating dock); both of privileged background, although Fletcher Moulton kept her desperately short of money; both, by 1897, locked in solitariness. Elspeth aspired to write. In 1888, she had published a novel of working-class life, of which she knew virtually nothing, called *Amelia Jane's Ambition*. In her large, looping handwriting, she wrote facile verse, routinely rejected by editors and publishers. By the time she met Kenneth Grahame, Elspeth Thomson was treading water, in need of stimulus, distraction, a focus. Kenneth too. Inspiration for the stories in which he rekindled his childhood had virtually run dry. By the end of the year, he had all but completed the pieces that make up *Dream Days*. Only 'A Saga of the Seas', in which the narrator briefly professes interest in the trajectory of married life, and the valedictory 'A Departure', were written in 1898.[19] For the better part of a decade, the process of fictionalizing memory in print had enabled him to return to an edited, imaginative remembering of former happiness. Its loss – the discarding of a lifeline – posed significant challenges.

But Kenneth had escaped entanglement before. It seems likely that he had repulsed Annie Grahame; firmly he held at bay the 'Bandersnatch', Evelyn Sharp. In Kensington Crescent, Tom Greg's salt-glazed stoneware and *grès de Flandres* tankards had been replaced by Kenneth's growing collection of children's toys, among them mechanical figures like a cardboard-limbed model acrobat called Leotard, 'who lived in a glass-fronted box... iron-jointed, supple-sinewed, unceasingly novel in his invention of new unguessable attitudes', and a drawer full of dolls.[20] As always, Kenneth looked backwards as well as forwards. Fear as much as curiosity coloured his contemplation of marriage. As he wrote in a poem called 'Love's Reveille', about fear of romantic commitment, 'the troops of Eros waver,/ See the ranks begin to shake!/... the little cowards break'.[21]

In the period preceding his wedding to Elspeth Thomson

on 22 July 1899, he misunderstood the force of her determination; too late, he recognized that the feelings he had
encouraged in her could not be ignored. She clung to her
attachment to him. Her pursuit was single-minded and
unwavering, by turns assertive and submissive, pathetic,
frustrated, loving. For a while, physically attracted to her,
drawn by her whimsy and flattered by her admiration,
Kenneth succumbed. And then he fell ill, and the game
became one-sided, and Elspeth scented victory.

· 9 ·

'I hardly feel I tread the earth
I only know that thou art mine'

A PPROPRIATELY, IT WAS a courtship of words. By letter Elspeth requested that Kenneth 'save thy heart for me'.[1] In his letters Kenneth offered her the devotion and physical ardour that gripped him intermittently. He committed himself by letter, too.

And what letters they were. Early on, Elspeth affected rusticity – 'Zur, Plaze to vorgive that I make so bold as to write-ee' – like a milkmaid or serving wench in a sentimental comedy; then her side of the correspondence disappears.[2] Kenneth wrote to her in a mixture of music-hall Cockney and baby talk: his letters are studded with childish mispronunciations, contrived spelling mistakes and elongated Cockney vowels, all conveyed phonetically. In this mawkish Darby and Joan play-acting, Kenneth was 'Dino', Elspeth 'Minkie', the grounds for these aliases now lost. It was not always a smoothly loving exchange: Kenneth's letters betray exasperation as well as fondness. If Elspeth had slackened her chase and Kenneth been less kind and decent, he would certainly have slipped away.

He was promoted early in 1898 from acting secretary of the Bank of England to secretary. It was an administrative and executive role, concerned not with devising policy but overseeing its implementation and, bar the dilatoriness of his approach, ideally suited to Kenneth's good-natured tact, his common sense and the respect his lack of partisan politicking had already won for him. Laconically Kenneth described his role as 'writ[ing] letters... for one's daily bread'.[3] At the end of the year, to a second chorus of praise, John Lane issued *Dream Days*. The book consolidated Kenneth's literary renown. His finances were comfortable, his position in the City assured.

Against this backdrop of professional and literary success, Grahame was enduring rapidly escalating ill health and feelings bordering on panic. 1899 proved crunch time. No record survives of Kenneth and Elspeth's meetings over the previous year and a half: that there had been communication, contact, advances offered and accepted is clear from Elspeth's behaviour subsequently and Kenneth's letters. Elspeth's single remaining letter contains a steely warning: 'Now 'ee don't think o' me, do 'ee? Happen he forgets the garden and all that stood in't... But he spook kine [kind], and the trees heard ee, and *I remember*.' [my italics][4] In February, Kenneth experienced a recurrence of the old familiar bronchial problems in the form of a severe cold. Elspeth fell ill at the same time. From his bed, he wrote her his first Dino/Minkie letter. He thanked her for a copy of *Moby-Dick*, admitted that he felt 'orfle slack still but am wearin down the cold grajjly', that he was lonely and low in spirits; he called her 'darlin', described himself as 'your own luvin Dino'.[5] Pet names and loving expressions

A riverside picnic in *The Wind in the Willows*,
Ernest Shepard's vision of Kenneth's rural idyll.
The febrile, escapist happiness of Kenneth's childhood
years at The Mount remained with him lifelong.

Kenneth as a new boy at St Edward's School, Oxford, c.1868, a 'sullen, reluctant, very ordinary-looking youth of nine summers'.
(*St Edward's School, Oxford*)

Kenneth in the uniform of volunteer infantry regiment the London Scottish, the stiff swagger of his posture belied by a hunted, uncertain expression.
(*Frederick Hollyer*)

Kenneth c.1895, on the surface a very eligible bachelor of respected position in the City and growing literary renown.
(*Getty Images*)

Frank Dicksee's 1881 portrait of Elspeth Thomson shows a young woman of cultured tastes and, behind doe eyes, steely fixity of purpose.

(National Trust / Bridgeman Images)

Kenneth and Elspeth's only child Alistair, known as Mouse. The angle of his head in this romantic photograph effectively conceals from view a debilitating squint.

(From Patrick Chalmers biography of KG)

Kenneth's relationships with both Elspeth and Mouse included their measure of tension. On good days, like the creatures of Kenneth's fiction, father and son walked for miles across the country surrounding Mayfield and Boham's.

Kenneth in his fifties by John Singer Sargent, retired from the Bank of England, the author of best-selling, much-loved stories.

(Lebrecht Authors / Bridgeman Images)

This photograph by Lady Ottoline Morrell depicts a snowy-haired, elderly Grahame, happier walking alone than at home with Elspeth or in the company of friends.

(© National Portrait Gallery, London)

Arthur Rackham's illustrations to *The Wind in the Willows*,
like this scene of Badger, Rat and Mole, were the last the artist
completed, published in 1940, the year after his death.

(The Stapleton Collection / Bridgeman Images)

'I love these little people, be kind to them,' Kenneth told
Ernest Shepard in 1930. Shepard's version of animals
and landscape has proved enduring.

Toad, Mole, Badger and Rat: Kenneth's multiple
diffused self-portraits, and a vanished world of
pre-war, pre-lapsarian certainties.

indicate the distance travelled since that first accidental meeting in Onslow Square.

Kenneth complained at the prospect of returning to the bank. 'Don't like goin ter work tmorrer one bit. It dus seem a shame wen I can do nuffin so well & other people aint no good at it torl.'[6] Take away the Cockney baby talk and it is the rhetoric of his 'Stevensonettes' about laziness: 'Loafing' and 'Of Smoking'. He gave in at the beginning of April. He put in a long day, culminating in a formal dinner. It would be his last day at work for five months. His cold was not beaten; pneumonia set in; he was suffering from empyema: pockets of pus in the lungs caused by bacterial infection. An operation was necessary, followed by convalescence at home in the care of his sister Helen. In the background, Sarah Bath hovered attentively. Kenneth's condition was serious, even life-threatening. For weeks Dino wrote no more to his Minkie. But Elspeth was every bit as attentive as Sarah Bath. To Kensington Crescent she brought carnations and grapes; the following month, with Kenneth no longer in danger, she suggested her stepfather send him port to build up his strength. Helen concealed her visits from Kenneth.

Helen's attitude was more than that of a nurse shielding her patient from disturbance. From the first, her antipathy to Elspeth was pronounced, and remained so. In an understatement, Kenneth described her as 'irresponsive' on the subject of his relationship: she disliked Elspeth on sight as a threat to Kenneth's independence and the family status quo. Helen is unlikely to have minced her words. She forbade Kenneth to write letters, Elspeth her target. At the end of May, Kenneth did so in secret: 'a smuggled line – for I'm not supposed to sit up writing letters yet', he explained.[7] Less covertly, he thanked John Fletcher Moulton for the port. Neither Elspeth's request to Moulton, nor Kenneth's letter of thanks, prepared the older man for revelation later of the exact nature of the relationship between his stepdaughter and the banker-writer. When it happened his reaction was much like Helen's. In the meantime he offered Kenneth the use of his carriage for restorative drives.

Kenneth invited Elspeth to spend the afternoon with him at home on 26 May 1899. He was under no obligation to do so and the invitation can only have been prompted by a desire to see her. It was an incendiary request, even more so as Kenneth arranged it secretly, when Helen would be out of the house finalizing plans for the trip brother and sister were about to make to the West Country to complete his recovery. Of course Elspeth accepted the invitation. In doing so, she accepted what, in 1899, amounted to a statement of intent on Kenneth's part, as he himself must have known. The invitation was a request that Elspeth jeopardize her reputation for him: on no other terms could unmarried young men and women spend time together alone, unchaperoned. Kenneth's invitation was tantamount to a proposal. Elspeth Thomson had hooked her fish.

Landing her catch would prove a different matter.

Kenneth's journey with Helen reminded both of their earlier convalescent holiday on the Lizard. For ten days they stopped in Torquay, 'rarver shut in and I wants the open sea and the roll o' the billers', in the first of the daily letters Kenneth wrote in pencil to Elspeth. His bedroom had a balcony, shaded by an awning; it overlooked the harbour, 'so I sees the botes'.[8] Even in such pretty surrounds a claustrophobic drama was beginning to unfold: Helen delighted at the distance between Kenneth and Elspeth, Elspeth concerned at loss of influence, Kenneth beholden to neither, unpredictable, elusive. Elspeth wrote bossy, possessive letters. Kenneth replied with childish prickliness – 'I eets wot I chooses and wot I dont want I dont and I dont care a damn what they does in Berlin thank gord I'm British' – or else a determination, at odds with his usual kindness, to make her jealous, the uncharacteristic impulse in itself a sign of his muddled feelings.[9] 'I don't want to be muvvered just now. If I do theres a chambermade wot'll take it on... Don't care much bout the otel... [We] shall move on nex week unless sumfin ideal in chambermades turns up.'[10] His grouchiness subsided in the absence of hectoring. He commended one of Elspeth's letters for its lack of 'preechin'.[11] And once, encouragingly, he involved her in a typical escape fantasy: 'I wish you were here we wood go crors the bay in the little steem ferry bote & not cum back – there is poppies t'other side.'[12]

From a distance, Elspeth was struggling. If the clandes-tine meeting at Kensington Crescent had felt conclusive, subsequent missives were anything but. She despatched presents to Devon, including hampers of food and a parasol that Kenneth called 'the tussore-silk umbrella'. She did her best to whet his appetite sexually, too, conjuring pictures of lovers in country lanes, arms encircling waists. His replies were confusing (probably because he was confused himself). He responded to one letter, in which she imag-ined them spending the night together, with details of the chambermaid's pink-and-white spotted dress. If Elspeth were with him now, he told her, he could 'play' at throwing her over the cliff, and she could play 'at bandonin me art-lessly for nuther'.[13] An exasperated, uncertain Elspeth over-looked possibly murderous tendencies and accused him of taking no interest in her physically.

Kenneth's replies were inconsistent. First he pushed

Elspeth away, then he reined her back in again. It might have resembled clumsy coquetry, but the letters lack convincing playfulness. Even his chosen patois of infantile Cockneyisms feels more like a form of concealment – a screen to hide behind – than a shared joke. Kindness balanced discouragement and disparagement often enough to avoid an out-and-out break. From Teignmouth he wrote a genuinely tender letter, assuring Elspeth that 'very soon we shall actually be tryin to be good to each uvver sted o writin it, which is sumfin to fink bout, and I'm sure I fink bout it orlwis my deer'.[14] Lamenting his broken sleep patterns, he added, 'then I fink of you – ony dreemings better as then I'm in reel Poppyland were wonderful things do appin!'[15] Whether Kenneth meant that his dreams were full of Elspeth and that she was with him in 'Poppyland', or that dreams of Poppyland – another escape fantasy – were better than thoughts of Elspeth is not clear.

In the face of all this to-ing and fro-ing, Elspeth clung doggedly to the inevitability of his capitulation. There is no reason to doubt her love for Kenneth. Nor had he provided categorical grounds for her to conclude that he did not reciprocate her feelings *in some measure*, even if he appeared incapable of straight talking or the flowery protestations of devotion that she really craved. After arriving in the Cornish fishing town of Fowey, he took to addressing Elspeth by the name of whatever boat in the harbour had most recently caught his eye: an ambiguous tribute. He also teased her that he was pleased to be sleeping in a single bed again, 'a nice narrer sorft one insted of a broard ard one that leadeth to destruckshin'.[16] To complete this picture of sexlessness, he inquired 'oos lookin arter my drorful o dolls at ome & givin em seed & water & grounsle?', his manner that of an exacting child.[17] Against this he told her that one of her letters had 'fired my ot young blood'.[18]

And then, wonderfully for Elspeth, something in him apparently changed. 'I play at your bein ere, oneymoonin, and corl it our "poppy-moon" cos it's a dreemmoon,' he wrote to her, 'and I only ope the reel will be in so nice a place.'[19] Days later he signed off a letter 'wif orl the love that's goin bout ere, from your most luvin Dino'.[20] He joked about Helen, her lack of humour, her unrelenting vigilance – a symbolic shift in his loyalty. He sent Elspeth a Battersea enamel box painted with a loving motto: 'the senkyment [sentiment] and spellin is irreproachable', he reassured her.[21] Happiness moved Elspeth to verse: 'Now of light there is no dearth/ Oh radiant warmth, and bliss divine/ I hardly feel I tread the earth/ I only know that thou art mine.'[22] Meanwhile Kenneth braced himself to confront Moulton. Even though he continued to refer to Elspeth in boating terms, his letters must have pleased her: 'I'm ritin to your farver today cos I think it wos time you was "brort to your bearins".'[23] There remained gaps in their knowledge of one another, Kenneth even unaware of her Christian name. He called Elspeth 'Elsie': 'So glad you're called "Elspeth",' he wrote, 'cos I didn't no it and I like it so much. Shant call you nuffin else.'[24]

To Kenneth's letter, a furious John Fletcher Moulton made no response at all. For the moment, Elspeth's assertive younger brother Courtauld was equally unforthcoming. Grudgingly, after an interval of silence in which Kenneth suggested elopement, Moulton relented. Kenneth waited until Helen had gone to visit friends to announce their engagement in the *Morning Post*. It was the first Helen knew of it and her reaction, on her return to Fowey, mirrored Moulton's. She repacked her suitcase for London. But the deed was done. After weeks of prevarication, Kenneth had resolved the impasse by the only means available to him, given that afternoon in London and his essential fair-mindedness. His regret was swift. In response to his question as to whether he really meant to marry Elspeth, his only answer was 'I suppose so; I suppose so.'[25]

Briefly in his letters to Elspeth, he hid behind talk of wedding presents. 'My bruvver ses ees got us that rare article – a reely decent biskit-box, moddled on a old

Georgian caskit so praps we shant arter swop orf that un';
he noted that, from her own friends and family, Elspeth
was 'cumulatin a large orde of bullion'.[26] Then two weeks
before the date set for the wedding, he panicked. 'Darlin,
ow'd you like ter go on livin at Ons: Sq: & cum away wif
me fer week-ends?... It wood be so nice & immoral.'[27] But
Elspeth had no intention of becoming Kenneth's wife part-
time or, worse, his mistress.

Kenneth's letters to the woman who was now officially his
fiancée were, if anything, more exasperating than those
that preceded them. Airily, he instructed Elspeth to take
charge of wedding plans and 'arrange wot is best for bofe of
us'. Then he filled his days with messing about in boats on
the Fowey River, or, with an idea of smoking as a means of
reinflating his recovering lung, 'smokin and drinkin o gin
and ginger beer' in a Fowey pub called the King of Prussia.[28]

He described Fowey in *The Wind in the Willows*, 'a little
grey sea town... that clings along one steep side of the harbour', with white-painted houses along the harbour side
and green seas lashing the headland. It is the last stopping
point of the seafaring rat in 'Wayfarers All'. The rapture of
the rat's description is Kenneth's own, his impressions of
sunshiny high summer in the weeks before his wedding.

MATTHEW DENNISON

'Through dark doorways you look down flights of stone steps, overhung by great pink tufts of valerian and ending in a patch of sparkling blue water. The little boats that lie tethered to the rings and stanchions of the old sea-wall are gaily painted... the salmon leap on the flood tide, schools of mackerel flash and play... and by the windows the great vessels glide, night and day, up to their moorings or forth to the open sea.'[29] Kenneth attributed the decision to marry in Cornwall to Elspeth.[30] Undoubtedly it suited his own inclinations and convenience better.

He had made new friends during the protracted con-valescent period in which, from a distance, he tugged and jangled Elspeth's feelings. 'Q' was a journalist and novelist, Arthur Quiller-Couch, exiled from London for reasons of his health, four years younger than Kenneth, a dandy and a passionate sailor, the son of an amateur folklorist. A trio of Cornish novels predated his arrival in the small town, including *Troy Town*, in which Troy is Fowey. He was married – Kenneth called his wife Louisa, whom he disliked, 'Mrs Q' or 'Qette'; they had a son and daughter, Bevil and Foy. Among his boats was a skiff, the *Richard and Emily*, which he loaned to Kenneth for sculling. Q organized sailing expeditions and picnics; he invited Helen Grahame, too. Paddling the *Richard and Emily* up and down creeks – slowly, mindful 'that I woon't stroke in a eight' [sic] – Kenneth amassed material that, a decade later, contributed to the composite river portrait at the heart of *The Wind in the Willows*.[31]

Through Q, Kenneth met Edward Atkinson, called 'Atky', commodore of the Fowey Yacht Club. He described their shared tastes as 'boats, Bohemianism, Burgundy, tramps, travel, books and pictures'; he might have added bachelordom.[32] Quiet himself, Kenneth relished Atky's talkativeness: 'ee flow on like summer brook,' he told Elspeth.[33] In Atky's house were a collection of forty-five telescopes, an 'enormous stock of clocks, barometers and binoculars' and 'a drore full of toys wot wound up', like Kenneth's drawer of dolls in London; lunch consisted of 'fancy hors d'oeuvres and every sort of sausage'.[34] House and owner attracted Kenneth like magnets. 'I get my boat at Whitehouse Steps and scull up the river past the grey old sea wall, under the screaming gulls, past the tall Russian and Norwegian ships at their moorings, and so into Mixtow Pill, and ship my oars at the little stone pier, and find Atky waiting on the steps, thin, in blue serge... and stroll up the pathway... to the little house above it, and be talking all the time and always some fresh whimsicality.'[35] Together Kenneth, Q and Atky staged a race of the wind-up toys in Atky's drawer: 'a fish, a snaik, a beetle wot flapped is wings, & a rabbit'.[36] Elspeth's response to such questionable larks does not survive. Her irritation that, their engagement formalized, Kenneth had retreated further into a *Boy's Own* world of sailing, loafing and penny toys was well founded. She did not suspect her indebtedness to Q, whom she correctly identified as a rival and resented on principle even before her arrival in Fowey on 21 July, the eve of her wedding. But it was Q who had pressed Kenneth to the sticking point, insisting that he owed Elspeth redress, and shown him by example the happy, fulfilling, boyish side of marriage.

In the end, Kenneth was married from Q's house, The Haven, above the ferry slipway, halfway up the hill away from the tiny town centre – woken early in the morning by a hurdy-gurdy player organized by his best man, Anthony Hope Hawkins. Elspeth wore an old muslin day dress with a daisy chain around her neck. At sunrise she had left the Fowey Hotel to watch the view. She remained staring on the dewy grass, listening to gulls, soft breezes playing in her hair, and decided against unpacking her smart, London-made wedding dress. She wore no engagement ring either. Nevertheless, at forty, Kenneth's bachelor life was over.

In place of the £5,000 settlement Courtauld Thomson had anticipated his stepfather bestowing on his older sister Elspeth, John Fletcher Moulton gave her just £250. It was Uncle John Grahame all over again.

· 10 ·

'I wish – Oh how I wish – I had married an Indian half-breed'

MARRIAGE DISAPPOINTED ELSPETH Grahame. Sex was her first complaint, and Kenneth's coldness. She did not keep her disenchantment to herself. Within a matter of weeks, she wrote to Emma Hardy, married to the writer Thomas Hardy, by 1899 a wife thwarted, saddened, overlooked, misused. Emma's response was predictably dampening. 'I can scarcely think that love proper and enduring, is in the nature of men... Love interest, – adoration, and all that kind of thing is usually a failure... *Hundreds* of wives go through a phase of disillusion – it is really a pity to have any ideals in the first place.'[1]

Kenneth was no happier than Elspeth. For him there was no element of surprise. An obsessive fear of sex had preoccupied him from the moment he committed himself. 'Once married I will try & be frankly depraved, and then all will go well,' was his peculiar response to a letter congratulating him on his engagement: it reads as if he is desperately trying to convince himself.[2] His final letter to Elspeth before she left London for Cornwall was a heroic attempt to impress upon them both the strength of his physical ardour: 'Don't sorst [exhaust] yourself cos its a long journey down & I want ter do the sorstin of you wen you gets ere – so you've goter save up fer your luver my pretty oos awatin of you ere.'[3] Elspeth's mistake was to believe him.

Perhaps at the time of writing, Kenneth had meant it. He was no stranger to sexual fantasies. His description of Charlotte's misbehaving dolls in a story called 'Sawdust and Sin' indicates at least imaginative familiarity with sex: 'Rosa fell flat on her back in the deadest of faints. Her limbs were rigid, her eyes glassy.'[4] Sadly, Elspeth, at thirty-seven, with her smart London clothes, her pet poodle and her lady's maid in attendance, lacked the robust earthy allure of Coralie or Zephyrine or a chambermaid pert in her starched, pink-spotted frock – symbols of straightforward boyish lust. All Kenneth's other fantasies of women cast them in untouchable storybook parts as fairies, princesses or enchantresses. Insofar as he was interested in sex at all, his taste took no account of the actuality of Elspeth's body. His desires were polarized: exoticism or celibacy. Sexual fantasy for Kenneth was another form of escapism – like his explanation later of the attraction of cinema: 'it is not exactly the sort of life we daily lead; and as we stroll homeward across the starlit common, towards our farmhouse, vicarage or simple cottage, we think "I wish – Oh how I wish – I had married an Indian half-breed!"'[5] Even at her most fey, Elspeth Grahame offered none of the imaginary excitements of an 'Indian half-breed'. As his friends mostly recognized, Kenneth had made a mistake in marrying at all. His instincts were those of a bachelor, even his perfunctory attitude to sex. He had no interest in Elspeth emotionally and little physical curiosity. He was happier 'finding oneself immersed in *Treasure Island* for about the twentieth time' or dreaming he was with Zephyrine and her ilk, 'riding the boundless Sahara, cheek to cheek, the world well lost', barricaded – by fear, habit or inclination – in a child's view of adult relations.[6]

In London at the end of the summer, Kenneth returned to bank duties. He took a long lease on a house in Kensington, 16 Durham Villas: until the time came to move in, he and Elspeth lived at Bailey's Hotel. Sarah Bath did not come with him from Kensington Crescent; she had declined to work for Elspeth. Elspeth set about transforming Durham Villas into a version of the Onslow Square house, complete with a crowded social life of the sort she had organized until recently for her stepfather. 'Don't never make me goter nuffin no more will you Minkie speshly wot they corls Kornversazshionies,' Kenneth had written to her before they were married.[7] Elspeth ignored him.

Their marriage scarcely outlasted their honeymoon of a handful of days in St Ives. Neither chose to record the cause of its pell-mell collapse. Kenneth recoiled from Elspeth, then he withdrew within himself. Sex was probably at the bottom of it; a combination of distaste, fear, even astonishment. In the house in Durham Villas, they embarked on parallel lives. Kenneth established a retreat in his study. 'It looked like a nursery,' a friend remembered. 'Books there were certainly, but they were outnumbered by toys. Toys were everywhere – intriguing, fascinating toys which could hardly have been conducive to study.'[8] The contents of the doll drawer at Kensington Crescent had overflowed into this cluttered stage set, where Kenneth escaped into make-believe to reconstruct his shattered innocence. Elspeth's exclusion was cruel. She was every bit as unsuited to adult life as he. Although she mistook Kenneth in key ways, she had always understood his idealization of his own version of childhood. She had even written him a poem, in which she wished she were four years old and he playing with her like a doll, a gauche attempt to present her own adult desire childishly:

> You should pinch my cheeks, and take
> Me in your arms, or on your knee
> Like some big doll, that would not break
> Think what a plaything *that* would be.[9]

The only playthings Kenneth craved were inanimate. Afterwards he claimed of his writing, 'In my tales about children, I have tried to show that their simple acceptance of the mood of wonderment... is a thing more precious than any of the laboured acquisitions of adult mankind,' but he did not intend to share with Elspeth the wonderment at which he laboured, and his determination that wonder belonged to childhood, before husband and wife met, inevitably pushed her from him.[10] Marriage revived his craving for solitude, like the narrator of 'The Roman Road' and for the same reasons: 'when the sense of injustice or disappointment was heavy on me, and things were very black within'.[11] At least he was sufficiently fair-minded not to blame Elspeth for a mistake that was mostly of his own making. It was disappointment, not perceived injustice, that overwhelmed him in the months following his wedding.

Elspeth maintained appearances by entertaining. Beyond invitations to a handful of literary associates, including John Lane and his wife, Kenneth appears to have done little to ensure that her efforts succeeded. His 'mind was not ruled by ordinary conventions. He made little attempt at small-talk,' a guest remembered. Given his literary celebrity, excuses were made for him. 'His silences were curiously companionable; & presently the thought would flow... He was a good – sympathetic – conversationalist because he was genuinely interested in the person he was talking to & in the latter's views as in his own. Never a great talker in a mixed company, he would sometimes give utterance to his least conventional sentiments with genial but unhesitating conviction.'[12] For the socially minded Elspeth, the combination of unorthodox views and silences in women's company must have been extraordinarily irritating.

Her unhappiness was acute, and contained its measure of recrimination. Unlike Kenneth, who had recognized his error in marrying Elspeth even before her arrival in Fowey, Elspeth had successfully buried any misgivings, only to find them swiftly exposed to the light. In her disillusionment she resorted to verse. Despite its indifferent quality, it accurately reflects her state of mind. Her poems tell a story of a couple entirely at odds; they paint a picture of a husband unconcerned by his wife's suffering. She describes 'cruel eyes whose radiant light/ Has cast a shadow as of night/ Over my heart, yet all the while/ Have no remorse, but sleep and smile.'[13] The bitter, waspish 'It would provoke a saint' points to an unbridgeable divide: 'If I should sigh, ah then you smile,/ And when I smile you sigh,/ But if I cry you laugh the while,/ And when I laugh you cry.'[14] Common to all the poems is the extent of her incomprehension. Despite Emma Hardy's gloomy fatalism, Elspeth was not yet ready to give up on the marriage for which she had fought so hard. 'I'm quite sure if you only knew/ How often I say that I love you/ Then you would believe my words are true/ For ah I do, for ah

I do,' she wrote, as if she could recapture Kenneth's heart with sincerity.[15] Time and again optimism failed her. In a poem called 'Rejected', her suffering is irreparable; she is the archetype of the spurned lover, condemned to endure miserably: 'The heart that thou hast broken no longer is mine/... Though my life's over alas I must live.'[16] She underlined the final line on the typescript of a poem she called 'Give me a kiss that will last for ever': 'That the force of remembrance may vanquish regret'.[17] It was a variant of Kenneth's borrowings from Marcus Aurelius, stripped of any real expectation of solace. Remembering was cold comfort: her memories taunted her.

But Elspeth would gain one blessing, at least, from her failed marriage. Within weeks of her honeymoon, she found herself pregnant.

Alistair Grahame was born on 12 May 1900. He would be Kenneth and Elspeth's only child and they called him 'Mouse'. They were unsuccessful partners and unsuccessful lovers; they would become unsuccessful parents.

He was born prematurely. Kenneth described him at birth as 'a big fellow & very good': he was blind in one eye, and had a squint and was part-sighted in the other.[18] Elspeth found childbirth traumatic and the baby's disabilities, as they revealed themselves by stages, more traumatic still. The reactions of husband and wife overlapped: Kenneth ignored and Elspeth denied Mouse's shortcomings. Instead they chose to consider him remarkable. For a time they persuaded themselves and anyone who would listen – and afterwards, Mouse too – that this was indeed the case. In doing so, they encouraged him to become a show-off; like Toad, he exulted noisily in his own exploits, 'all conceit and boasting and vanity... and self-praise and... gross exaggeration'.[19] As a child he was a bully and a prig, given to patronizing the servants and fighting small girls ('ee not only smack them but dig is ten fingers deep into their tender flesh', Kenneth reported unblushingly to Elspeth[20]). He lacked the 'pleasant sort o way with him' that Kenneth had attributed to the Boy in 'The Reluctant Dragon'. Once he was old enough, self-discovery proved painful. His birth did not resolve the deep fissures in his parents' marriage, and a miniature of Elspeth painted by her sister during Mouse's infancy shows a tired-looking, fluffy-haired woman struggling to smile. Instead, the child became a focus for unfulfilled longings, an antidote to disappointment. From birth he carried a weighty burden.

Even by contemporary standards, Kenneth and Elspeth played a limited part in Mouse's upbringing. For Elspeth, nervous collapse followed new motherhood, a sofa-bound

semi-invalidism. At some point before 1904 she undertook
the first of a series of residential cures at Woodhall Spa in
Lincolnshire. Her illness was never clearly identified, but
treated by both Elspeth and Kenneth with utmost gravity.
Her doctors forbade even the effort of writing letters; they
prescribed neck exercises, sulphur baths and cold soup
with cream. To a friend, Kenneth described her as 'a Living Skellington'.[21] He himself indulged the weakness in
his chest with journeys abroad, beginning with a trip to
Marseilles in 1902 on which, despite his ailments, he ate
'a perfectly whacking and stupendous quantity of bouilla-
baisse'; he travelled without Elspeth and never considered
taking Mouse.[22] In 1904, en route for Spain, he went to
Paris with Atky, like Q one of Elspeth's bugbears. In this
hypochondriac ménage, Mouse spent much of his time
alone with his Dutch nursemaid, disparaged by Kenneth as
'Gnädige frau flat-foot'. There are suggestions that the boy
felt isolated. When his nurse explained to him that 'next
of kin' meant 'your nearest and dearest', he replied, 'Then
I suppose in my case the next of kin is the canary.'[23] Aged
four, Mouse was stricken with severe peritonitis while
staying with distant cousins of Elspeth's. Elspeth was at
Woodhall Spa, Kenneth in the Pyrenees. Throughout his
lengthy convalescence at the seaside in Broadstairs, his
parents were intermittently absent. Mouse did not tell

them that, when the condition was at its worst, he saw visions of Christ, 'my Friend... the Carpenter... He came to see me and sometimes I would go and talk to Him'.[24]

Elspeth's hagiographic attitude to her son offered her an outlet for the torrents of affection that Kenneth had rebuffed; she considered him a child of the 'elfin-celestial sort', born for some 'high purpose'.[25] Her mythologizing began in Mouse's cradle and stubbornly resisted all contrary evidence. How far she believed her hyperbolic claims at first is impossible to say. She was certainly capable of persuading herself of almost anything that held despair at bay, and she continued to trumpet her son's perfections to the grave.

· 11 ·

'There was a story in which a mole,
a beever, a badjer and a water rat
was characters'

F OR KENNETH, MOUSE'S birth began the slow process of his return to writing. Since the publication of *Dream Days* in 1898, he had virtually stopped. His memories of The Mount were all written out, his equilibrium unbalanced by illness and the terrible misjudgement of his marriage, his mental dualism fully occupied with the bank and the room full of toys. In 1899 he wrote an introduction to a new edition of Aesop's Fables, including two brief fable parodies of his own, 'The Ape and the Child in the Leghorn Hat' and 'The Dog, the Child and the Moon'. Both adopt the animal's viewpoint. It wasn't much to show for a year, albeit his clear preference for the animals rather than the children in his stories foreshadows the child-free *Wind in the Willows*. Two years earlier *The Academy* had described him as a 'clear-thinking, exuberant prose artist, content to wait for the visitation of his muse'; for a period the muse appeared to abandon the toy-filled study in Durham Villas.[1] But fatherhood rekindled selective memories of Cunningham Grahame, of lochside walks and poetry and tall tales of adventure, of Longfellow's 'long, long' thoughts of youth. While Mouse was still very young, Kenneth embarked on a series of stories of his own devising that brought father and son close together. His purpose appears to have been no more than the boy's entertainment.

To Elspeth, Kenneth described a wintry afternoon in Kensington Gardens in 1903: 'There was a story in which a mole, a beever a badjer & a water rat was characters & I got them terribly mixed up as I went along but ee always straitened them out & remembered wich was wich... I erd him telling [Nurse] artewards "and do you no... the mole saved up all his money and went and bought a motor car!"... You will perceive by this that Mr Mole has been goin' the pace since he first went his simple boatin spedition wif the water rat.' In this instance Mouse had requested the story-telling: 'once e ad got is mouf well stuffed wif brednbutter ee sed softly "now tell me about the mole!" So the ole of the time I ad ter pin out mole tories [spin out mole stories]'.[2] Mouse begged to be taken to the Serpentine, which he called 'the river'. 'Suppose ee fort it was river wot mole and water-rat got upset in,' Kenneth told Elspeth.[3]

The journey that ended in *The Wind in the Willows* had begun within three years of Mouse's birth: his reference to 'Mr Mole', a boating expedition with a water rat and an upturned boat points to stories told even earlier. From the beginning, key elements were in place. Five years would elapse before publication. In the interval, Kenneth resigned his position at the Bank of England and the Grahames left London for life in the country, close to The Mount and within reach of the Thames. *The Wind in the*

Willows is a book that has changed the lives of countless thousands of readers. It changed Kenneth's life most of all.

The beginning of 1905 dragged heavily. January invariably inspired 'a certain amount of run-down-edness', with the result, Kenneth wrote, that 'I shirk my work – set & look at it & swear orfle but not do it.'[4] His pleasure in bank business had always been intermittent: his letters read oddly for a senior figure in the City of London. With age and worsening health his position as secretary had come to inspire anxiety and a corrosive self-doubt. A dream he described in a story written for Mouse reflects his continuing discomfort in the world John Grahame had chosen for him. At a great City banquet, he wrote in the third person, he 'dreamt that the Chairman actually proposed his own health – the health of Mr Grahame! and he got up to reply, and he couldn't think of anything to say! And so he stood there, for hours and hours it seemed, in a dead silence, the glittering eyes of the guests – there were hundreds and hundreds of guests – all fixed on him, and still he couldn't think of anything to say! Till at last the Chairman rose, and he said "He can't think of anything to say! *Turn him out!*"'[5]

Mouse was in Broadstairs, recuperating at length from his operation for peritonitis in September. Elspeth had joined him, though she stayed separately at the Albion Hotel and, later, in a house called King's Mead overlooking the sea. For weeks on end, Kenneth was alone in Durham Villas. He was looked after by Eliza Blunt the housekeeper, a gamekeeper's daughter described by Elspeth as 'big and solid'; he still expected Elspeth to micromanage even the most trivial domestic details, like ordering new tins of tooth powder for him.[6] He wrote to her every day in the familiar combination of baby talk and Cockney: on paper and at a distance they were Dino and Minkie still. At intervals there were flashes of candour. 'Detestable time o year, this – not take "no joy" in ennyfink,' he wrote in February.[7] Kenneth missed Mouse more than Elspeth; he missed their stories together: 'It teem to trange [seems so strange] not to ave him arst wot the mole & the water rat did anuvver day.'[8] With no writing to occupy him, he poured the childlike alter ego he had previously distracted with his Olympians stories into Dino's fractious missives.

He relaxed in the company of a London neighbour, an artist called Graham Robertson. Today Robertson is best remembered as the subject of a striking portrait by Sargent, preternaturally youthful and enveloped in an enormous greatcoat. He was a wiry, thoughtful, dog-loving aesthete – Sargent painted him with his eleven-year-old poodle, Mouton: through his work as a theatre

designer was a friend of Henry Irving and Sarah Bern-
hardt. Kenneth coveted his collection of drawings by
William Blake. A shared belief in fairies connected the
men. 'We would discuss the points of view, proclivities
and antecedents of [Fairyland's] inhabitants with all the
passionate earnestness displayed by really sensible people
when speaking of... Lunch Scores or Cup Finals,' Robertson
remembered.[9] In 1908, the Grahames were in the audience
of his successful play, *Pinkie and the Fairies*, starring Ellen
Terry. The men shared conservative, as well as whimsical,
instincts: outside London, Graham Robertson lived in a
cottage without electricity or mains water. For Kenneth
his companionship was undemanding – like that of Sidney
Ward, Tom Greg, Q and Atky; much of their time together
passed silently. His verdict that Kenneth 'had a marvellous
gift of silence' echoes Q's admiration for his 'silences that
half-revealed things beyond reach of words'.[10] Robertson
considered his friend out of place in London. 'In London...
he looked all wrong. As he strode along the pavements one
felt to him as towards a huge St Bernard or Newfoundland
dog, a longing to take him away into the open country
where he could be let off the lead and allowed to range
at will. He appeared happy enough and made the best of
everything, as do the dogs, but he was too big for London
and it hardly seemed kind of Fate to keep him there.'[11]

It was a view akin to Kenneth's own. Insistently, Kenneth's thoughts toyed with abandoning the capital for good. For ten weeks the previous summer, at a cost of five guineas a week, he had rented a cottage from 'a strateforward rather silent man, who didn't tempt to puff is ouse in any way or ignore defects': Woodside, in South Ascot, in a clearing backed by pine trees and close to a building plot earmarked for a new Roman Catholic church.[12] Kenneth went there with four-year-old Mouse, whose reaction to the quietness, the dark shadows of the trees, and the loss of Kensington Gardens and the Serpentine was one of listlessness. The landscape delighted Kenneth, despite the building plot. 'I'm sure you understand,' he wrote to Elspeth at Woodhall Spa, 'that it is not *house* I in love wif, but *situashun* – ouse is small, and we may ave to put up with minor inconveniences.'[13] It was the latest instance of his intense engagement with place, and the small house in the trees' shadow offered respite from anxious discontent.

It was not quite time to leave London, however. Pressing reasons precipitated Elspeth's return. Some years earlier, her brother Courtauld had discovered that John Fletcher Moulton had withheld from both Elspeth and their sister Winnie their share of their mother's estate, a sum in the region of £600 each a year. Fletcher Moulton denied everything, wriggled, refused to make restitution. He counted without his stepson's tenacity. While continuing to share the house in Onslow Square, Courtauld brought a civil action against his stepfather. Fletcher Moulton responded with 'a small but very highly paid army of KCs'.[14] Less expensively, Courtauld organized his sisters' counsel; on Elspeth's behalf, he liaised with Kenneth rather than communicating with her direct. The court hearing was repeatedly delayed. At each suggestion that she testify, Elspeth relapsed into nervous shock. Once she suffered 'acute inflammation of the tissues of the neck'.[15] Eventually, in April 1905, the case was heard. Elspeth's testimony was a startling account of borrowing from the butler and the cook to make good the shortfall of Fletcher Moulton's meanness. As Kenneth had anticipated, her settlement did not come close to the back payment of around £11,000 which he had calculated as owing. After legal expenses, Elspeth received about £2,500, equivalent today to more than £200,000.

That summer, with Elspeth mostly recovered, the Grahames took their first family holiday. They travelled to Inveraray. Given the unhappiness of his previous return in the summer of 1866, Kenneth's choice is surprising, and he swiftly regretted it. To Q he wrote cryptically that Scotland 'had gone down-hill considerably since I was there last – anyhow I didn't care about it'.[16] Ghosts of the past jostled. Although he had seen and heard nothing of his father from the age of eight, and excluded him from his writing, Cunningham's shadow lingered: Kenneth had offered Mouse a bribe of £100 if he avoided alcohol until his twenty-first birthday. In the evening he continued his bedtime stories of 'a Badger... a Mole, a Toad, and a Water-rat, and the places they lived in and were surrounded by'.[17]

The Grahames' final departure for the country took place the year after, in 1906. In the short term, they kept on 16 Durham Villas as a pied-à-terre for Kenneth until his resignation from the Bank of England. Their destination was the place John Grahame had chosen for his niece and nephews forty years ago, after Bessie's death and Cunningham's downfall. In Cookham Dean, on high ground above the larger Cookham-on-Thames, Kenneth had easy access to that stretch of the river between Pangbourne and Marlow that provides most of the setting for *The Wind in the Willows*. His beloved Oxford lay within reach, with its fair at the end of the summer and gentlemen's outfitters and the Covered Market where he bought ties and 'Oxford' sausages 'without any skins on their poor little persons'.[18] Elspeth described the village romantically as 'so far removed from civilization... that the inhabitants, who were mostly of gypsy origin, were known as "the mountainy men"'. She dismissed them fretfully as 'a lawless brood'.[19] For the first time in his life, Kenneth would have the use of a boat house and a boat of his own. He also acquired a very fat black Berkshire pig, his favourite domestic animal, and called it Bertie.

· 12 ·

'It's much more sensible to pretend
the world is fairy-land than an
uninteresting dust heap'

LIKE BEATRIX POTTER'S *The Tale of Peter Rabbit*, which Kenneth read aloud to Mouse, *The Wind in the Willows*, begun orally, took shape in a series of letters. As with Potter's story, a governess preserved the letters; encouragement by a third party nudged him towards a full-length book. In the case of *The Wind in the Willows*, Mouse was the child, Naomi Stott his governess, appointed in 1905, Constance Smedley the winning American who cajoled Kenneth back to his desk.

A separation provided first impetus. In the late spring of 1907, Elspeth persuaded Kenneth to go away with her on his own, leaving Mouse with Miss Stott. She chose Cornwall; she may have intended a second honeymoon after years of illness. Claiming poor health one more time, Kenneth again abandoned his bank duties. Mouse and Miss Stott set off for seven weeks of sea air at Littlehampton. Afterwards Kenneth returned to London and Durham Villas and the bank. Missing Mouse, he wrote to him from Falmouth, Fowey and Kensington, lengthy letters that begin with 'Toad's Adventures since he was dragged off to prison by the bobby & the constable' and end with a banquet at Toad Hall and, 'to his great satisfaction', Toad 'an object of absorbing interest to everyone'.[1] Eventually the fifteen letters amounted to first drafts of chapters VIII, X, XI and XII of *The Wind in the Willows*.[2]

Constance Smedley's decision to approach Kenneth in mid-August, when, as she remembered rosily, 'the mists of early autumn were invading hedge and lane', included its measure of serendipity.[3] In Fowey, Kenneth had befriended a visiting American businessman, Austin Purves. By letter, Purves introduced him to President Theodore Roosevelt. Roosevelt's admiration for Kenneth's writing was unqualified: in June the president told him how much he wished he would visit the States as his guest at the White House; he requested signed copies of *The Golden Age* and *Dream Days*. By the time of Constance Smedley's arrival, uninvited, on the Grahames' doorstep, having driven over from neighbouring Bray, not only had Kenneth plotted much of Toad's story in his letters to Mouse and maintained for some time his bedside narrative of Mole, Rat and Badger, but his predisposition in favour of appreciative American readers was roundly positive. Constance Smedley was a writer herself, a feminist, attached to the well-funded Philadelphia-based *Everybody's Magazine*. The magazine's editor, John O'Hara Cosgrave, rated *The Golden Age* and *Dream Days* as his 'ideal of literary charm'. At Cosgrave's request, Miss Smedley's mission was to persuade Kenneth to produce more of the same for publication in *Everybody's*. She was not the first person tasked with such an undertaking since the appearance of *Dream Days*, and she would certainly have failed had it not been for the existence of the Toad letters to Mouse.

Luck and astuteness were on her side. She introduced herself to Kenneth as a relation of the governess in *The Golden Age*, whose name she shared; she avoided any mention of her feminism. Together they discussed her novel *An April Princess*, which Kenneth and Elspeth had both read. Kenneth doubtless approved its heroine's statement, in response to a criticism that she is behaving like a child, that 'it's much more sensible to pretend the world is fairy-land than an uninteresting dust heap'.[4] It was his own philosophy to the letter. Although Kenneth seemed to her 'as remote and shadowy as the countryside' and 'encased in the defensiveness which dreads coercion', her visit stretched to several hours, long enough to overrun Mouse's bedtime.[5] Eavesdropping on Kenneth and Mouse, she overheard 'an unending story, dealing with the adventures of the little animals whom they met in their river journeys'.[6] She suggested the stories form the basis of a new book. Kenneth demurred; she did not contradict him. 'He hated writing; it was physical torture. Why should he undergo it?'[7] Later he expanded: 'There is always a pleasure in the exercise, but, also, there is always an agony in the endeavour. If we make a formula of those two motives, I think we may define the process. It is, at best, a pleasurable agony.'[8] Miss Smedley pointed out that the book was virtually written already. Her visit was the first of several. She took the opportunity to outline her plan to an enthusiastic Mouse. It was to Constance Smedley that Kenneth explained about the sharpness of his recall from the ages of four to seven, an indication that this determined, intelligent but romantic young woman had succeeded in winning his confidence. 'Coming back here wakens every recollection,' he told her.[9] To his own surprise, Kenneth found himself agreeing to her scheme.

He wrote much of *The Wind in the Willows* in London that autumn of 1907, adding new episodes about Mole, Rat and Badger. He wrote last the chapters that were most personal, 'The Piper at the Gates of Dawn' and 'Wayfarers All'. The first sums up in iridescent prose the rural pantheism he had begun exploring in print two decades earlier. Kenneth's benign, half-smiling Pan figure, 'the Friend and Helper', appears to Rat and Mole in an awe-inducing vision of glowing sunlight, aspens and roses, and returns to them the lost otter cub Portly. In 'Wayfarers All', Rat battles the siren call of the South, symbol of adventure and escape. His is a vision of another sort: a hallucination, momentary madness. 'Two or three chapters were new to me and come as charming surprises,' Graham Robertson wrote to Kenneth.[10] The men had discussed the book during writing, including Kenneth's concern over an appropriate title. 'It may come – as you say – while shaving,' Robertson attempted to reassure him; his own suggestions included 'The Lapping of the Stream', 'The Whispering Reeds' and 'River Folk'.[11] A surviving manuscript is headed 'The Mole and The Water Rat'. Significantly Kenneth did not discuss his extra chapters with Robertson, although there are affinities between the visionary quality of 'The Piper at the Gates of Dawn' and drawings by Blake. Such was his certainty that he had no need to.

But there were surprises in store for Kenneth, too. Despite Constance Smedley's enthusiastic admiration, *Everyman's Magazine* turned down the novel. At The Bodley Head, John Lane also rejected it. Kenneth's literary agent, Curtis Brown, attempted to place individual chapters with magazines, like the earlier Olympians stories: he failed as well. It was not an animal fantasy that publishers wanted from Kenneth, but a third volume of stories of Edward, Selina, Charlotte and Harold. Eventually, and with reservations, Methuen & Company accepted the manuscript. In place of an advance, Curtis Brown negotiated 'excellent rising royalties', for which Kenneth would have reason to be grateful.[12] Methuen advertised the book as *The Wind in the Reeds*, the same name as a collection of verse by

Yeats, and commissioned a single illustration by Graham Robertson. How, or by whom, the final change of title was made went unrecorded.

It proved a depressing year. That summer, Kenneth resigned from the Bank of England. 'The responsibility was a great strain & was telling on his health,' Elspeth wrote to Austin Purves's wife, Betsey, in a careful piece of whitewash.[13] Kenneth's modest pension award of £400 per annum, formalized in a letter of 2 July, gives credence to rumours at the time that his decision was forced upon him: he may have fallen foul of the bank's new governor, William Campbell Middleton, or a bullish director called Walter Cunliffe. His colleagues' expressions of regret emphasized his personal qualities in place of any particular prowess. His departure followed swiftly. By the end of July Elspeth was able to tell Betsey Purves, 'we've disposed of the lease of the London house'.[14] She described Mouse, but not Kenneth, as 'quite charmed' with Cookham Dean; he had learned to play chess; Kenneth had given him a pair of rabbits, called Peter and Benjie after the stories by Beatrix Potter.

Publication of *The Wind in the Willows* in October was as much a damp squib as the conclusion of his thirty years at the bank. Reviews were overwhelmingly negative. 'As a contribution to natural history the work is negligible,' claimed the *Times Literary Supplement*; it criticized the absence of an 'animating spirit'.[15] Kenneth's venture into new territory provided chief grounds for reviewers' carping and sales were initially poor. With Elspeth, Kenneth retreated to Devon, where he caught flu. By the middle of December, he told Austin Purves, 'the after weakness and general grogginess still continues, and I can only walk a mile or two, and then an armchair and slumber till dinnertime, which is a nuisance'. He described himself as '"in a moment of depression"', the inverted commas perhaps a sign of his embarrassment; it was true, nevertheless.[16] The next month, still unnerved by what he interpreted as his double failure as banker and writer, Kenneth referred to 'a moment of some stress and pressure in my private affairs'.[17] 'I have given up the City of London altogether,' he wrote. 'I am still somewhat unsettled.'[18] A letter from Roosevelt brought momentary cheer, as did their meeting later in the year, in Oxford. 'At first I could not reconcile myself to the change from the ever-delightful Harold and his associates,' the President told him. 'Now I have read it and re-read it, and have come to accept the characters as old friends; and I am almost more fond of it than your previous books.'[19] In February, with Elspeth, Kenneth escaped gladly for three months to Switzerland and 'the northern part of Italy, for colour and anemones and Chianti and so on'.[20] Feelingly he had written to Purves, 'I want to go on my travels with a light heart.'[21]

The Wind in the Willows tells a story about animals living in, on or around a riverbank. Kenneth's reprise of *Three Men in a Boat*, it is also a novel about fellowship and companions, and Kenneth might have appended to it the old Water-rat's assertion in Oscar Wilde's 'The Devoted Friend', of 1888, that 'love is all very well in its way, but friendship is much higher'. It is concerned with rootedness and concepts of home. It celebrates an idealized rural society and ideal bachelor leisure, glimpsed in Toad's inventory of 'everything you can possibly want': 'biscuits, potted lobster, sardines... soda water... baccy... letter-paper, bacon, jam, cards and dominoes'.[22] It is about stability, indeed a manifesto for maintaining a certain status quo that is presented as an idyll.

It is an aggressively conservative book and its targets include socialism and any form of faddishness or craving for novelty, Toad's weakness. Loyalty to caste and suppression of the masses are at the heart of its patrician creed. It is triumphantly an exercise in denial, written within a decade of the First World War at a moment when death duties, agricultural slump and left-wing political philosophies had begun an onslaught on inherited privilege that sure-footedly gained in momentum as the century progressed. Its charms include lyrical descriptive writing and nostalgia: even on first publication, *The Wind in the Willows* was nostalgic. It is a book for readers of all ages, and it appeals to the instinctive conservatism of small children who hanker to preserve their particular worlds intact.

It is also, despite Kenneth's stringent denials, pre-eminently an autobiographical book. It emerged from the disaster of his marriage to Elspeth and in the aftermath of an attack on the Bank of England in November 1903, in which a lunatic assailant called Robinson turned a revolver on Kenneth and fired three times, missing on each occasion. ('Mr Kenneth Grahame is wondering what is the meaning of the expression, "As safe as the Bank of England",' *Punch* commented; Kenneth was not amused.) This incident formed the coagulant for all Kenneth's fears of social unrest: he recycled it in Toad's encounter with a ferret sentry at Toad Hall, who 'said never a word, but he brought his gun up to his shoulder'.[23] The book reflects his joy in fatherhood and the intensity of his affinity with the natural world around him. It is a heartfelt repudiation of sex. Elspeth's later claim that she was the book's inspiration and catalyst was truer than she knew, though not for the reasons she reckoned.

Kenneth's description of the novel as 'free of the clash of sex' doubtless baffled his publishers who, in Edwardian England, would have expected nothing else of a book aimed even partly at a child readership and written by the author of *The Golden Age* and *Dream Days*. It is equally free of the clash of marriage and all but denies the existence of women. For Kenneth this absence of sex was intrinsic to the perfection of the Riverbankers' lives and to his own pleasure in writing. In discussing *The Wind in the Willows* he returned to it repeatedly. 'It was pleasant to write & especially – what people don't see – by simply using the animal, to get away at once from weary sex problems & other problems, & just do jolly things without being suspected of preaching or teaching.'[24] To President Theodore Roosevelt, an admirer of his Olympians stories, he explained the book's 'qualities, if any, [as] mostly negative – i.e. – no problems, no sex, no second meaning – it is only an expression of the very simplest joys of life as lived by the simplest beings of a class that you are specially familiar with and will not misunderstand.'[25] At best these are disingenuous interpretations, but Kenneth clung to them fixedly.

The Wind in the Willows rejects outright male–female relationships. That it does so deliberately is clear from Kenneth's comments, which seem to indicate how far 'weary sex problems' lay at the root of his own malaise. The main literary source for the story is Homer's epic account of Odysseus's ten-year return to Ithaca after the Trojan War, the *Odyssey*. *The Wind in the Willows* is the *Odyssey* rewritten in Kenneth's study full of toys, the one room completely free of Elspeth and the taint of Onslow Square. Toad is Kenneth's Odysseus, whom the Romans called Ulysses: the connection is made explicit in the book's final chapter, 'The Return of Ulysses'. Toad's adventures parody Odysseus's. Although he possesses echoes of Odysseus's cunning and his talent for disguises and deceit, Toad is heroic only to himself; Kenneth's is a mock epic with elements of satire. Odysseus is assisted by Athene and a bevy of obliging goddesses; Toad is rescued by 'a pleasant wench and good-hearted', a lowly gaoler's daughter. The home that Odysseus left behind is exposed to the depredations of a band of suitors, arrogant and unscrupulous men determined to win the hand of his wife Penelope. Uninvited, they consume all that Odysseus's estate provides, much as the inhabitants of the Wild Wood plunder Toad Hall and the contents of Toad's cellar. Odysseus's son Telemachus aspires to be like his father and share in Odysseus's renown; in Kenneth's story, the otter cub Portly is brought round to this point of view. Meanwhile, Rat is tempted by the seafarer, a version of Odysseus's encounters with Lotus-eaters and Sirens.

A single central element is missing from Kenneth's

rewriting: Penelope. A longing to be reunited with his paragon of a wife draws Odysseus across the 'wine-dark' seas, defying mortal dangers. There is no Penelope figure in *The Wind in the Willows* and, far from being voluntary, Toad's homecoming is forced upon him by Badger and his friends in order to restore the hierarchical order of their tiny social microcosm, a pyramidal structure with Toad at the apex. Shattered by his marriage to Elspeth, Kenneth was unable to incorporate within his story any approximation to selfless, life-enhancing love between men and women. Odysseus weeps for Penelope; Toad weeps for himself. As an omission it is deeply unfair. Elspeth's lifelong mourning of the love she thought that she and Kenneth shared reveals deep affinities with Penelope. Like Penelope, she lacked power to bring about a reunion; she too could only wait for her husband to come back to her. Instead, Kenneth resorts to coercion to return Toad to Toad Hall. As a member of the landed elite, Toad must recapture his ancestral acres to oust the creatures of the Wild Wood, members of the proletariat in the thinnest of disguises.

As with the boys in his Olympians stories, all four principal characters in *The Wind in the Willows* borrow features of his own; their makeup includes reminders of Furnivall, Henley, Q, Atky and, in Toad's case, Mouse. On the brink of his fiftieth birthday Kenneth completed a novel in which Toad's itch for adventure is defeated by Badger's respect for convention and common sense; strong forces of conformity thwart his hankering for escape. For Toad there can be no going it alone or evading the role society has allotted him: status imposes duties and responsibilities, a part to be played and a manner in which to play it. Rat's sudden wanderlust dimly echoes Cunningham Grahame's abandonment and perhaps Kenneth's own fantasy of leaving Elspeth; it is quashed by the sensible Mole. Like Kenneth, Toad and Rat are hostages to fortune, both trapped by the people who claim to love them best. Viewed from this angle, Kenneth's conclusion is bleak indeed.

· 13 ·

'The somewhat inadequate things that really come off'

A T FIFTY, DRESSED in his own version of the country-man's garb of tweed breeches and shapeless jacket, Kenneth remained physically imposing. 'He was very tall and broad, a massive figure, but with no spare flesh,' wrote American academic Clayton Hamilton. 'His hair was white, but his face was almost beatifically young, and he had the clear and roseate complexion of a healthy child.'[1]

He no longer felt either young or healthy, his winters invariably plagued by bronchitis or influenza, but it was not the move from Durham Villas to the country that disappointed him. Each morning he fed a tame robin with a currant, crumbs or a paring of cheese – 'It seems to me that the family is not complete without a tame robin,' Mouse wrote after its departure – and he awoke to 'a carolling of larks and a tinkling from distant flocks... the wind-hover hang[ing] motionless, a black dot on the blue'; over Quarry Wood he heard 'the sound of Marlow bells'.[2] For hours he walked. Often he was alone in the silence of his own thoughts, tracing sheep tracks 'or the foot-path through copse and spinney not without pleasant fellow-ship with feather and fur', up ghostly chalk paths to the summit of the Downs and the views he loved: 'the vale, with its clustered homesteads, its threads of white roads running through orchards and well-tilled acreage, and, far away, a hint of grey old cities on the horizon'; at home he ate heartily and smoked.[3] Instead a bigger disillusionment took hold of him in the immediate aftermath of leaving the bank and completing what would be his final book. Stubbornly it lingered. Cookham, like Inveraray, had fallen short of the picture he had padlocked in his memory. New houses of red brick marred its fringes. It was crowded and busier than he remembered. New developments had shattered 'its natural life of somnolency', and Kenneth, until recently a weekender from London, found himself a spectator, not a participant, in this authentic local world he prized so highly.[4] The lease on the Grahames' house, Mayfield, would shortly expire and the effort of house-hunting again so soon pressed on him. And yet his days were overwhelmingly empty. Casting about for an explanation, he described himself simply as 'somewhat stale and rusty'.[5] His marriage to Elspeth was no happier. 'Company too often means compromise, discretion, the choice of the sweetly reasonable,' he wrote later, a first-hand assessment of awful bitterness.[6] For lengthy periods he heard nothing of Atky or Q, who nevertheless dedicated his novel *The Mayor of Troy Town* 'to my friend Kenneth Grahame and the rest of the crew of the *Richard and Emily*'; Graham Robertson remained in London; for the moment Kenneth's relationship with his brother Roland was amicable rather than sustaining, and was dealt a blow by the death that winter of Roland's wife, Joan. As always, thoughts of escape into solitary make-believe taunted him, compounding gnawing regret. In *The Wind in the Willows* he had divided experience into 'the best and the raciest adventures', which occupied 'the category of what-might-have-happened-had-I-only-thought-of-it-in-time-instead-of-ten-minutes-afterwards', and 'the somewhat inadequate things that really come off'.[7] 'Everyone's experience will remind him that the best adventures of his life were pursued and achieved, or came suddenly to him unsought, when he was alone,' was his mature conclusion.[8] It was a dispiriting reflection for a man who was both husband and father.

In his introduction to *A Hundred Fables of Aesop*, written in 1899, Kenneth had joked that 'parents of the human species have an altogether singular and unaccountable method of rearing their young'.[9] So it had been in his own case: abandoned by Cunningham, treated with briskness by Mrs Inglis. Kenneth and Elspeth's approach to parenting had its unaccountable qualities too. They continued to spend lengthy periods apart from Mouse. In the summer of 1909, only months after their own return from Switzerland, the Grahames dispatched Mouse once more, with Miss Stott, to 'his favourite seaside resort – Littlehampton, a rather horrid little place, which he adores'. To Purves, Kenneth explained 'I wish our tastes in places were similar, so that we could be together.'[10] It ought to have been an unnecessary regret on the part of a devoted father of comfortable means, able to provide for his family whatever holiday they wished. On this occasion, Kenneth blamed an eye problem of Elspeth's, which forced her to avoid bright sunlight, though the summer had been notably overcast. There are signs that both parents found Mouse exacting company. His diet of inflated praise, Elspeth's encouragement of flamboyant precocity and Kenneth's laissez-faire attitude to self-discipline had wrought predictable results. In his last years at home before preparatory school, Mouse struggled, with limited under-standing, to live up to the towering expectations of his parents. He became bombastic and showy, this chubby boy who battled poor vision and crippling shyness; Kenneth called him a 'social animal', likening him to Elspeth rather than himself.[11] Towards Kenneth, Mouse was both loving and dismissive. He requested that his father address him as 'Michael Robinson', the name inspired by the gunman who had attempted to shoot Kenneth in the Bank of England. He divided adults into 'Goods' and 'No Goods', and shuffled his father between both categories. On happier days they explored the lanes and woods together; they visited a sheep fair; in the apple-loft belonging to a neighbouring farmer they sampled 'every sort of apple and filled our pockets

– and then we sat in the parlour and discussed circuses, and... agreed that they were the only thing worth living for', this father who idealized boyhood and his son, like the fictional Edward, on the brink of departure for school.[12] One walk brought them in the path of the hunt: Mouse was blooded by the huntsman and presented with the fox's brush. For hours each day he was alone with Elspeth, who continued to spend much of her time on a sofa sipping hot water and listening to the gramophone, so thin that she refused to be photographed and had given up the effort of anything resembling respectable dress. With terrible consequences for Mouse, she embedded herself in a world of sentimental fantasy – despite, or because of, the collapse of her relationship with Kenneth.

In the late spring of 1910, neither of his parents involved Mouse in their choice of a new house. 'It seems funny to call Boham's home,' he wrote from another of his parent-less holidays, 'so when chaps ask me where my home is I tell them Berks because I have not seen Boham's.'[13] The house in question was a modest thatched red-brick Tudor farmhouse named after its first owners, a family by then extinct and '[a]sleep in a row in the churchyard'.[14] It stood in the village of Blewbury, a 'little grey old-world Berk-shire village, in King Alfred's country, probably much as it was 1,000 years ago'.[15] Farmhouse and village enchanted

Kenneth. Rapturously he described 'a plain Berkshire farmer's house, "unfaked" and unaltered, with no special architectural features, with its orchard on one side and its farm buildings on the other'.[16] Close by wound a trout stream. In a pig trough Kenneth discovered a handsomely carved William and Mary chimneypiece; indoors, workmen stripping away layers of paint revealed linenfold-panelled oak doors 300 years old. Kenneth converted a barn into a study, though his writing days were all but over; he installed electric light and a bathroom. It took months to settle in properly, he in one part of the house, Elspeth quite separate in another, with an ex-soldier and his wife to look after them. Kenneth hung pictures; with hammer and tacks he fitted carpets; he arranged his large collection of Sailor's Farewells. Once the barn had bookcases and a stove, he surrounded himself with 'beautiful old Italian china, [De] Morgan tiles, Hispano-Moorish platters, old Capo di Monte figures, and what not of rare and lovely specimens of the ceramic arts'.[17] 'Peasant toys from all countries' intrigued Constance Smedley when she visited.[18] Kenneth admitted they had 'too much stuff for so small a space', but went on collecting, including Staffordshire animal figures, miniature tea services for dolls and eighty-five pieces of 'old glass most delicately and minutely engraved in sporting subjects, hounds, stags, birds'.[19] He soon became 'perfectly well aware that every time Mr Lay [a neighbouring farmer] thrashes out a rick, some non-paying guests... seek admission to the house', and he acquired a cat.[20] Kenneth applied himself to village life to the extent of Sunday church attendance, though he accepted few of the Anglican orthodoxies. He had written out his belief in a rural pagan god in nature in 'The Piper at the Gates of Dawn'.

In London, in his first years at the bank, he had escaped at weekends, fleeing the capital's 'ignominy of rubble and brick-work', delighting in the big open spaces of the Downs and a conviction of his own place in nature's jigsaw. Then his walks had inspired his writing, 'for Nature's particular gift to the walker, through the semi-mechanical act of walking... is to set the mind jogging, to make it garrulous, exalted... certainly creative and suprasensitive.'[21] Now he no longer craved inspiration. In *The Golden Age* and *Dream Days*, he had relived a version of best aspects of his childhood; *The Wind in the Willows*, a dialogue with himself, contained a personal creed that solidified with the act of writing. Although a pall hung over him, his joy in nature endured. Away from Cookham's new red brick, the expansive country thrilled him with its ancient unchanged pastoral rhythms. It is his own delight that he attributes to Mole in 'the harvest... being gathered in, the towering wagons and their straining teams, the growing ricks, and the large moon rising over base acres dotted with sheaves'.[22] To a visiting American he eulogized 'this "antick" corner of Berkshire, so near everything by train and yet so very remote in historic time'; he told Austin Purves 'it is only about 54 miles from London, but 5,400 years remote from it in every way'.[23] In his walks, he sought out shepherds and their stories of husbandry; he found '*intoxicating*' a local sheep-fair, 'the noise of dogs and sheep and dealers, the procession of sheep and men, the droves of flockmasters and dealers in the most fascinating clothes you can conceive'.[24] His imagination responded to animals and plants in as lively a fashion as four decades earlier, drawing crocodiles in the margins of a book. 'I like most of my friends among the animals more than I like most of my friends among mankind,' he admitted to one friend.[25] And his solitary progresses were meditative. Answering a request from Curtis Brown, he promised 'to go forth once more on the Downs and give it prayerful consideration among my friends the hares and plovers'.[26]

He wrote to Graham Robertson to persuade him to take a cottage nearby.[27] His instincts were mostly reclusive, as if he recoiled from a world by which he felt thrown over. His visits to London, usually for a matinée, were fleeting. With the exception of his letters to Austin Purves, he scarcely wrote to friends. 'I fancy that professional writers nearly all hate letter writing,' he offered by way of excuse.[28] Even to Purves, he wrote only a fraction of the letters he intended. 'I *do* write you any quantity of truly magnificent letters,' he protested. 'In my armchair of evenings, with closed eyes, or strolling in the woods of afternoons – or with head on pillow *very* late on a thoroughly wet and disagreeable morning. I see my pen covering page after page.'[29] Most of the letters went unwritten. Kenneth was battling debilitating inertia from which he never recovered. With no pleasure in their marriage, husband and wife let slip domestic standards too. Constance Smedley described Kenneth's careful dressing of a salad, 'the occasion a lovely intimate ceremony', and sloe gin decanted into antique glasses, but on the pantry shelves mice nested unchecked.[30] The Grahames gave up dressing for dinner, and Elspeth firmly set aside her smart London wardrobe. In her hand-knitted stockings and shabby cardigans, she had become an ill-kempt wraith, this woman who formerly played hostess to writers and politicians – Tennyson and Tenniel, the Asquiths and Campbell-Bannermans. Behind her back, villagers sniggered at her eccentricities. She had become domineering; her conversation was strident and hectoring. In small ways she bullied Kenneth. For reasons that have not survived, she forced him to wear special underwear that was changed only once a year.[31] She had developed a streak of meanness, despite her settlement from Fletcher Moulton, Kenneth's pension from the bank and healthy royalty payments from *The Golden Age*, *Dream Days* and, after an unpromising beginning, *The Wind in the Willows*. From her sofa she continued to write verse, including the poems she asked Constance Smedley to deliver to Thomas Hardy in the autumn of 1907, which Hardy judged 'charming'.

Kenneth's appetite for writing had not deserted him completely. At the end of July, he received a proposal from publishers A&C Black. It was an invitation to rural escapism and fitted exactly his instincts of the moment, a book of 'anecdotes, folk-lore, philosophy, political economy, botany, ornithology, and references to anything and everything that rambles in beautiful English country are likely to bring to mind'.[32] Remembering the successful progress to book form of his Olympians stories published in the *National Observer* and *The Yellow Book*, Kenneth requested that *Highways and Hedges* appear chapter by chapter in instalments, like a serial. Editor Gordon Home agreed. He offered Kenneth a single payment of £50, with no royalties. And so the scheme foundered – and with it the last book that Kenneth might have written.

· 14 ·

'Noble ideals,
steadfast purposes'

IN MAY 1911, Mouse 'made the great plunge'.[1] Two years later than Kenneth, he embarked on boarding school life.

The Old Malthouse was at Langton Matravers, 'a nice place in Dorsetshire, near the coast, with beautiful bathing and surroundings', a new school run by Rex Corbett who, in 1903, had captained the England football team.[2] From experience Kenneth knew enough of boys' schools to be apprehensive on Mouse's behalf. At first his fears proved groundless. Used to protracted separations from his parents, Mouse settled quickly. Despite Corbett's own sporting prowess, the school was not excessively hearty and Mrs Corbett was a benign, motherly figure. As at every previous juncture of his life, Kenneth and Elspeth did not press to see Mouse often. A month after term began, he wrote to his parents that 'nearly every boy in the school is going home for the corination [sic] [of George V on 22 June 1911] so there will be only 5 left here including myself.'[3] If it was a request that they take him away, it fell on deaf ears. Instead Kenneth contributed to the cost of Blewbury's coronation decorations and lamented that 'owing to the coronation... all the village fetes and fairs have been fixed for as late in the summer as possible, to give us a chance of saving a few more pennies for shows and roundabouts'.[4] Mouse's reward was to be a summer at home of sweltering heat, two months without rain and 'crops burnt to a fierce tawny red'.[5]

Before term began, Kenneth and Elspeth had taken him to Cornwall. Over a number of weeks they visited the Lizard, then Fowey. The idea was Kenneth's. 'I want Mouse to make the acquaintance of my Cornish haunts, and friends, before he goes to school – then he may like to go back there,' he explained.[6] Kenneth's letters offer no indication that he any longer associated Cornwall with his wedding to Elspeth. His concern was to introduce Mouse to Rat's joy of 'messing about in boats'. He wanted him to meet Atky and Q, and Q's son Bevill, at the age of eight page boy at Kenneth and Elspeth's wedding, known as 'The Boy', an archetype of handsome, affable, athletic young manhood, an unrealistic object of emulation for the clumsy, short-sighted Mouse. Atky's house, with its crowded collections of nautical instruments and bibelots, its gramophone records and '"special" luncheons', and Q's peacock manner of dress, impressed Mouse suitably. The Boy was mostly absent sailing. Mouse made friends with his younger sister, Foy. He delighted in the Lizard's 'sparkling air... and he liked the simple, friendly people who were all so nice to him and let him run in and out of their places, and had him to tea'.[7] In Cornwall he discovered the fascination of the sea. 'I think a stormy sea is one of the finest sights one can see anywhere,' he wrote to Kenneth later.[8] Kenneth's version of the holiday, preserved in a handful of letters, omits any mention of Elspeth. His focus was Mouse and his determination that Mouse share his attachment to Cornish places and people.

His time with the boy continued to throw up its challenges. Wittingly or otherwise, Elspeth had coloured Mouse's view of his father. Mouse's letters from school referred to Kenneth as 'Inferiority' or, less contemptuously, 'the Artful and Extravagant One'. In the autumn of 1911, Kenneth and Elspeth travelled to Brittany. Mouse directed at Kenneth, not Elspeth, his resentment at being left behind again. 'I hear that you have taken advantage of my absence to make a bolt for France, and I have no doubt that before long you will be in Gay Paris or Mòntécârló [sic]. I am at present staying in a little island known as England, of which you may have heard. You will find it on the map of Europe, to the west of France. Nothing doing here at present, England *is* a dull little place!'[9] As Christmas approached, Kenneth was still the target of Mouse's exactions: 'A warning to Inferiority. If he does not take me to the pantomime, and to Montecarlo, and give me three helpings of Xmas pudding and mince pies and otherwise show his paternal affection, well – I'll let him know it.'[10]

There were less combative interludes, too. Father and

son shared a taste for adventure stories. Kenneth sent Mouse copies of Dumas's novels. Mouse read *The Prisoner of Zenda* and, inspired by Hope's novel, indulged in extravagant Edward and Harold-style games in which he was Dirk Lawless 'the Bloody Buccaneer', while a friend called Jennings played Rupert of Hentzau. With evident forethought, his Christmas present to Kenneth in 1912 was a brass candlestick that he had found himself, 'said to be old, according to the shopkeeper'.[11]

Even the kindly regime at the Old Malthouse could not disguise Mouse's limitations. At their best, his letters display charm, lively curiosity, a buoyant sense of humour and, occasionally, irony. He loved acting and swimming and poetry, choosing Tennyson's 'The Lady of Shalott' for his final recitations competition. Academically, the prodigy nurtured by Elspeth proved to be anything but. The Grahames had selected Rugby for Mouse's public school, a surprising choice given the handicap of his partial-sightedness, his ungainly lack of athleticism, his mixture of self-consciousness and the preciousness instilled by Elspeth, his 'strongly introspective mind' focused on himself, his disdain for his peers.[12] Instinctively Mouse recognized Common Entrance as a challenge and dared look no further. Cloud-like, it overshadowed his final year at prep school. The examinations fulfilled his misgivings.

He described them as 'a most strenuous time... afterwards I was as limp as a wet rag. I know I did not do myself justice, and feel certain I shall not pass.'[13] His fears went unrealized, though his performance, as he suspected, was middling. 'It was good of you to telegraph about the exam,' he wrote to Elspeth. 'I was so thankful to pass at all, that I did not mind passing so near the bottom. So long as you are satisfied with the result, I am sure I am.'[14] As his parents surely realized, Mouse was growing up. No trace of the Toad-style triumphalism that had armoured him hitherto colours this sad little note. For Alastair Grahame at thirteen, beginning to apprehend a gulf between his parents' admiration and outsiders' verdicts, there was trouble on the horizon.

As Mouse braced himself for gathering storms, Kenneth retreated into childhood. In a letter of 19 March 1913, A. R. Waller of the Cambridge University Press wrote 'to ask if you would be disposed to compile two small books of really good poetry for young children'.[15] He defined 'young children' as below 'lower forms of secondary school'. Kenneth's acceptance was swift but conditional. He rejected Waller's offer of £50 for the two volumes, requesting instead royalty payments of 10 per cent of the published price of a shilling, to which Waller agreed. He then worked on the project for more than two years, by turns enthusiastic and dilatory. Determinedly he fought John Lane over fees for poems published by The Bodley Head. To the man who had turned down *The Wind in the Willows*, despite a successful association of author and publisher spanning two decades, Kenneth's letters were polite but firm. In place of Lane's requested twelve guinea fee for a dozen poems, Kenneth negotiated a single payment of £7 7s. 'You shall have the poems at the price you name... You always get your way with me!' Lane replied, not quite truthfully.[16]

One way or another, Q hovered in the background. The previous year he had been appointed Edward VII Professor of English Literature at Cambridge. In the last decade he had published nine novels and edited a clutch of well-received anthologies, including the *Oxford Book of Ballads*. It may have been Q who suggested to the university press Kenneth as anthologist. Alternatively, Kenneth's acceptance was quickened by professional face-saving or a simple desire for occupation, and it was the thought of Q – so happily busy and successful – that stirred his inertia. Belatedly, *The Wind in the Willows* had won the plaudits denied it on publication. On both sides of the Atlantic it had achieved a tardy critical and commercial success that has continued ever since. But its buoyant fortunes did not inspire Kenneth further. He had described himself once as a tap, not a spring, and so it continued. 'He wrote what he wished when he wished and he wrote no more than he wished,' Grahame Robertson claimed, an assessment that is mostly accurate.[17] His writing was not the source of Kenneth's depression, although the right project, like *Highways and Hedges*, might have offered him respite. He had not shaken off the lassitude of the previous decade and his career foundered on inactivity. Measuring himself against the yardstick of energetic Austin Purves or Q, he felt his shortcomings acutely. His acceptance of Waller's invitation may have included a measure of relief.

He approached the task with something of his former high spirits. 'It is a bit of a score to get any Swinburne into a school book,' he told Waller, in an oblique reference to the poet's fruity reputation.[18] By December he could report, 'I have got my two little vols about three-quarters done, but am rather stuck for a little more matter, which I can't find to my liking, so I have been rather letting the thing slide.'[19] It slid for another year before the selection was complete and, in October 1915, Kenneth wrote his preface. With hindsight, it appears an overwhelmingly personal selection. He includes work by the poets he had first learned himself: Macaulay, Tennyson and Shakespeare; Robert

Herrick, whose poems he had noted in the ledger he stole from the Bank of England, and Wordsworth, whose view of a child's insight – at the heart of his Olympians stories – so closely resembled his own. On the shores of Loch Fyne, Cunningham had introduced him to Longfellow; Cunningham or Mrs Inglis or Annie Grahame may have drawn his attention to the Scottish author James Hogg. He also included two poems by Graham Robertson. His preface reiterates sentiments he had explored a lifetime ago in 'Stevensonettes' for Henley. He describes his selection as a 'wicket gate' into poetry's 'domain': this domain, of course, resembles an idyllic English landscape, 'with its woodland glades, its pasture and arable, its walled and scented gardens here and there... its sunlit, and sometimes misty, mountain-tops'. In a decision that reveals his attitude to his own childhood bereavements as well as the book's wartime context, he explains his exclusion of poems about death. 'Dead fathers and mothers, dead brothers and sisters, dead uncles and aunts, dead puppies and kittens, dead birds, dead flowers, dead dolls... I have turned off this mournful tap of tears... preferring that children should read of the joy of life.' It was the spirit of optimistic denial that had shaped his fantasies at The Mount and which ripples through his stories in *The Golden Age* and *Dream Days*. For Kenneth, as for generations of readers since, 'the joy of life' was the message of *The Wind in the Willows*.

It proved a commodity in short supply for Mouse, who left Rugby after six intensely miserable weeks. Kenneth blamed his fellow new boys, 'a roughish lot'.[20] Q blamed Elspeth and recommended instead home tutoring or a day school. No one blamed Kenneth, though he had ignored Q's coded warnings and, in the character of Toad (public property since publication of *The Wind in the Willows*) provided grounds for ragging of the son who inspired and resembled him. Elspeth set her sights on Eton. 'It is useless to conceal that, to persons of the rather indeterminate age of Mouse and myself,' wrote Old Etonian Graham Robertson, 'boys between twelve and sixteen are a little trying as companions.'[21] In Robertson's letter was an inference Kenneth chose to ignore: that Mouse was unsuited to the company of his contemporaries. He concluded lamely, 'any boy can have a passable time at Eton if he has a good temper'.[22] It was encouragement enough for Elspeth, who subsequently précised his letter as 'everyone was so eager we should try Eton as affording the greatest *contrast* to Rugby'.[23] If Kenneth challenged his wife, he was overruled. To Eton Mouse was dispatched, in January 1915. He took with him pictures for his room drawn for him by Graham Robertson, including an illustration of parachuting mice, and 'everything in [Kenneth's] power to buck him up... & anything that could hearken & help him', chiefly pocket money and tuck.[24] A year later he left, after what was probably a nervous breakdown. Elspeth switched tack and found a tutor, a Mr Dall, in Surrey. She told her brother 'he is they say really a gentleman & very particular whom he takes'.[25] But it would be a year before Mouse was well enough to leave Boham's or contemplate further study.

In the meantime, husband and wife occupied themselves with war work and the privations of wartime living. They had lost their ex-soldier servant and his wife. Six months elapsed before replacements could be found. Interim village help was of the 'rough and untrained' variety with predictable results: 'the garden of course had gone to pot, and the house was dirty and disordered'.[26] With his work on the *Cambridge Book of Poetry for Children* complete, Kenneth, a veteran of the London Scottish, joined Blewbury's Volunteer Defence Corps. In the last letter he wrote to Austin Purves, who died in February 1915, he described evening drill practice 'in a beautiful great timber-framed thatched barn – like my own, only three times as big. The rats run in and out of the thatch along the rafters, and the barn cat, who ought to be attending to them, sits on wheat sacks and reviews us with great delight.' Kenneth was elected commanding officer, apparently on the strength of his moustache: 'they said I was the most martial-looking of the crowd, and there I agree with them; they were careful to add, however, that it wasn't for any other reason whatever, and that also I can fully understand.'[27]

Mouse took riding lessons on the Downs, although his sight was deteriorating further. He kept up the lessons during his time with Mr Dall in Surrey, which suited him. On holiday in Somerset with his parents in the summer of 1917, he spent hours swimming on his own. He decided to join a volunteer regiment; the Oxford Cadet Corps was closer to home than a Surrey equivalent. For training purposes, the officer in charge overlooked the handicap of Mouse's vision. Kenneth discussed Mouse's future with Roland's stepson Keith Fieling, a don at Christ Church, Oxford. Their decision that he give up Mr Dall's tutoring and begin undergraduate studies at Christ Church in the Lent term of 1918 sped him to his third unhappy experience of institutional academia.

With Mouse absent again, Kenneth sank back into aimless days of fireside reading and long walks across the Downs. He replied to a handful of the letters about *The Wind in the Willows* that reached him from across the globe; Elspeth dealt with the remainder. Repeatedly he parried suggestions of a sequel. He knew that there could be no return to the riverbank now. Mouse's collapse, cast loose of the careful fictions of Boham's, and the muddy carnage of the war mocked his earlier vision. When, like Mole, Kenneth placed his ear to the reed-stems and 'caught something of what the wind went whispering so constantly among them', the song he heard was a new song. In 1913, he had offered the *St Edward's School Chronicle* an essay called 'The Fellow That Walks Alone', inspired by Caxton's legend of Edward the Confessor, 'the patron saint of all those who of set purpose choose to walk alone'.[28] The essay celebrated the 'emancipation... only attained in solitude' and complete withdrawal into 'the country of the mind'. It denied the camaraderie at the heart of the earlier book. Instead Kenneth raised funds for the French Red Cross; he gave letters by Thomas Carlyle and Harriet Martineau to a Red Cross charity auction at Christie's; he wrote quatrains for engraving on the lych gate that villagers erected in memory of Blewbury men killed in the fighting. To the French he attributed an appreciation of fellowship that he himself had passed beyond. 'There is no people in the world so quick and ready as the French to appreciate a word of spoken sympathy, a word of friendliness, a word of good cheer and encouragement.'[29] On his walks beside the river he looked out for water rats, whistling when he reached a spot where he expected to find one. Often there was no response.

Mouse's decapitated body was discovered early in the morning of 8 May 1920 on railway lines close to a level crossing near Oxford's Port Meadow. A coroner's inquest five days later delivered a verdict of accidental death. The position of the body and the nature of its injuries suggest suicide. After two years, his university career – the lodestar of Kenneth's life – ended in tragedy. He had failed examinations in Greek and Latin literature and Holy Scripture three times; he had failed to make friends; he had failed to resolve an introverted preoccupation with his own agnosticism and his pockets were stuffed with religious tracts.

He was buried on his twentieth birthday in Holywell cemetery, and the headstone erected by his parents celebrates in perpetuity the 'noble ideals, steadfast purposes and rare promise' that they had decided long ago were his defining qualities. On his coffin lid Kenneth scattered lilies of the valley.

· 15 ·

'The Fellow That
Walks Alone'

K ENNETH WROTE TO Curtis Brown on 29 April 1926 to quash suggestions that he embark on an autobiography. 'I have kept no diaries or memoranda at all, and since the War my memory seems to have gone all to pot. I doubt much if I could ever get as much as a bookfull together.'[1] Three months later, he was unable to answer questions about the bindings of early editions of his books sent to him by A. J. A. Symons, compiling a bibliography of the 1890s: 'I have to speak from memory, for my own library doesn't help me at all. I cannot find any early editions – I suppose I gave them away or they were given away for me.'[2]

The process of forgetting and discarding began in the wake of Mouse's death. For once, Kenneth and Elspeth's response to devastation aligned. Elspeth drew up a list of 'Articles for Disposal, the Property of Mr and Mrs Kenneth Grahame' for a firm of auctioneers. It included the 'collection of Bristol, Sunderland and Nailsea Glass of the Glass rollers known as "Sailors' Farewells", forty in number' that Kenneth had begun in Fowey in the weeks before their wedding. To local jumble sales she consigned Mouse's clothes. Boham's was let for eighteen months. On 30 October 1920, Kenneth and Elspeth left England for Italy and their first journey together to Kenneth's inspiring, restorative South.

Neither left any record of the next four years, spent mostly abroad, of their thoughts of Mouse, their feelings for one another, or the nature of their companionship in grief. 'If no earthly kingdom will our wistful hearts in peace unite,' Elspeth had written years before in a poem called 'Constancy'.[3] Intense unhappiness united their hearts more than any fumbling after love or even fondness ever had. They settled themselves comfortably in the Hotel des Princes, in Rome's Piazza di Spagna, their first destination, for a year. It was the Golden City of Kenneth's *Golden Age* stories and it offered him the only things his numbness craved: macaroni, fettuccini, porchetta, fresh anchovies and sardines, sweet potatoes, mortadella sausage, white Parmesan cheese, ice cream, marrons glacés, baskets of sweet biscuits, and omelettes cooked by an exiled Russian princess wearing diamond earrings and served by an archduke in a squalid side street of Mussolini's capital where 'socialists and soldiers continually shot at each other'.[4] Fountains everywhere charmed him with the sound of running water: the Fontana delle Tartarughe, with its carvings of tortoises, and the Trevi Fountain, where he sat at night alone, beguiled by reflections of moonlight in the splash and spray.

Members of the British and American ex-pat community left visiting cards at the Grahames' hotel. Elspeth told

Patrick Chalmers that she and Kenneth were in accord on not returning their calls. There were exceptions. In 1922, the British ambassador Sir Rennell Rodd invited Kenneth to address the Keats/Shelley Association. In a talk entitled 'Ideals', afterwards published in the *Fortnightly Review*, Kenneth returned to 'the fancy-realm of childhood'. 'Ideals' is simultaneously a confession and an apologia. It is not the waving arms of a drowning man, but his rubber ring, proof that Kenneth responded to Mouse's death as he had reacted to every vicissitude. 'When we are tempted to speak somewhat contemptuously of the wayward fancies of a boy, let us ask ourselves seriously whether we ever entirely lay aside this habit of mind; whether we do not, all of us, to the last, take refuge at times from the rubs and disappointments of a life where things go eternally askew, in our imaginary world where at any rate we have things for the time exactly as we want them?'[5] It was Kenneth's trusted escape mechanism, more dependable now than his own writing or Marcus Aurelius's stoic aphorisms. Its solace excluded Elspeth as firmly as the closed doors of his doll-filled study at 16 Durham Villas, or the barn fitted out with stove and bookshelves that he had left behind at Boham's.

From Rome the Grahames visited the Dolomites, Rapallo, Lake Garda, Capri, Sicily, Florence and Siena. Dressed in an Inverness cape, Kenneth walked alone through the varied landscapes, as he walked the rises of the Downs. With Elspeth he visited picture galleries and churches, admiring triptychs and altarpieces by the Italian Primitives he had first encountered in London. 'I have walked through hundreds of picture galleries in my day, always with pleasure and interest, often with the keenest delight,' he remembered, but the only souvenirs he kept lifelong were 'tiny shells picked up from some Cornish beaches, miniature fishing nets from Brittany... little gewgaws from foreign and English fairs of which he was a lover', like 'the Treasure Trove of some darling child', in Elspeth's words.[6] The tenant of Boham's, a Mr Davies, left in 1922, but still they did not return to England to order their affairs. Rome drew them back and back. 'We wintered in Rome, and summered there, and Eastered, and Christmas'd,' Elspeth said, 'and knew every one of the 490 old churches.'

Eighteen months after Mr Davies left it empty, in the spring of 1924, Boham's was sold and Kenneth and Elspeth returned to England. They had already dispersed much of the impedimenta of their marriage; they had given away Mouse's belongings. Elspeth kept boxes of correspondence, including letters sent to her by Kenneth from Cornwall in the summer they were married, and sprightly, courtly

Valentine's Day verses written specially for her by Sir John Tenniel. She kept Mouse's letters up to his departure from the Old Malthouse and discarded all evidence of his unhappiness afterwards. She kept the letters about *The Wind in the Willows* that Kenneth received from across the globe, to which she, rather than he, invariably replied. In this carefully edited private archive survived Dino and Minkie's love match, the myth of Mouse's charmed life and universal acclaim for the book Elspeth took credit for. Her culling and hoarding were her own equivalent of Kenneth's imaginative escapism, and equally misleading.

They chose a house close to the river in the large, bustling village of Pangbourne. Southeast of Oxford, with Oxford traffic clearly audible, it did not, like Blewbury, retain the shadows Kenneth once prized of King Alfred's ancient landscape. But its large garden contained a grassy amphitheatre that reminded him of a circus ring; there was a terrace for reading and *The Times* crossword; he hired garden help but no domestic staff, and refused to install a telephone. In Pangbourne, Kenneth accepted the role the village bestowed upon him of local littérateur. He gave talks in the Constitutional Hall; he introduced visiting speakers. When Osbert Sitwell lectured to the Pangbourne Art and Crafts Society, Kenneth used his introduction to lament the despoliation of the landscape. 'For as I pass through this beautiful world, always with an eye – I hope – for the beauty around me, year by year I see things I have admired and loved passing and perishing utterly.'[7]

It was a statement he might have applied more widely. Not only places but the people Kenneth loved were passing from him. Atky had drowned in a sailing accident in 1911; the Boy, Bevill Quiller-Couch, had tried in vain to save him. The Boy himself was dead, killed by Spanish flu in February 1919 after distinguished war service. Austin Purves, whose assiduous correspondence rallied Kenneth's morale after publication of *The Wind in the Willows*, had been dead for a decade. Kenneth had not seen Helen since his marriage to Elspeth, nor Roland following a disagreement in 1913. He felt no curiosity about new friends and his attempts to maintain contact with old friends were as half-hearted as ever. 'You are an elusive fellow,' an exasperated Q told him in 1925.[8] Once, Kenneth had told Elspeth, 'You *like* people. They interest you. But I am interested in *places*!'[9] His interest in Pangbourne was confined to its Thames frontage. His world had shrunk and the places that still engaged his attention were the countries of the mind he commended in 'The Fellow That Walks Alone' – above all the mythical river that Rat told Mole he lived by, with, on and in.

He had little appetite for novelty. He accepted a commission from J. M. Dent to write an introduction to the memoirs of a circus impresario who called himself Lord George Sanger; he declined the offer of an authorized biography of Dr Barnardo. 'It seems to me that the essay is somewhat remote from the book,' wrote editor Guy Pocock, after reading Kenneth's first draft of the Sanger introduction. 'It is also quite remote from the *man*.'[10] Characteristically, Kenneth had mostly overlooked Sanger. His essay revisits his own memories of circuses; it celebrates the romance of the travelling players' lives, glimpsed through the prism of Kenneth's conservatism: 'The show people are a contented folk, chiefly I think because they rarely want to be anything but what they are. They like the life for itself.'[11]

It was a wistful and double-edged statement, though Kenneth was too polite deliberately to invoke Elspeth's weaknesses in a manner recognizable to anyone but himself. A Pangbourne acquaintance described her in unlovely terms, 'a chinny woman of leathery countenance, who wore well-cut tailor-made tweeds and talked stridently and interminably, laying down the law about her preferences in literature and art, and never taking much heed of what anybody else had to say'.[12] He dismissed her 'wearing personality' and reported what was clearly village gossip: 'I gathered that Mr Grahame had long since learned that it was a waste of time and energy to attempt to express an opinion in his wife's company.' Village gossip also drew attention to the quantities of claret and champagne delivered to Church Cottage, which may have become essential to Kenneth. It contrasted with Elspeth's cooking, in which she gave free rein to well-honed instincts for parsimony and cutting corners.

As long ago as 1910, Kenneth had told a visitor to Boham's, 'Granted that the average man may live for seventy years, it is a fallacy to assume that his life from sixty to seventy is more important than his life from five to fifteen.'[13] It is a restatement of the old familiar theme: that with the end of childhood comes death in life. In his own case, his final decade has the quality of a recessional, which he perhaps anticipated. Most winters he and Elspeth returned to the Continent, usually Italy or Cannes. Through walled medieval towns, across broad, sun-soaked boulevards, he walked with a cane now, shoulders stooping, white hair lifted aloft by southern breezes, sometimes short of breath, touched by lumbago, a stiffness in his joints. He ate and drank too much and, in Pangbourne, chaffed Dr Bourdillon, who advocated restraint as an adjunct to treatment for arteriosclerosis. When Elspeth's back was turned he escaped Church Cottage in pursuit of ice cream.

Much of each day was devoted to reading: Browning, Tennyson, Boswell, Dr Johnson, Henry Fielding, Samuel

Butler, Robert Burns, Marvell, Herrick, Shelley and Shakespeare. He disliked the novels of the Brontës, this courteous, undemonstrative mid-Victorian whom Q described as 'eminently a "man's man"'.[14] He was still in thrall to the river, where he spent a part of every day, listening, watching, scenting the air like the small creatures he had immortalized. *The Wind in the Willows* itself was inescapable and he did not try to escape it. E. H. Shepard visited Church Cottage in 1930, preliminary to beginning work on a new series of illustrations. Kenneth told him, Shepard recorded, that he would like 'to go with me to show me the river bank that he knew so well, "but now I cannot walk so far and you must find your way alone"'.[15] He offered Shepard a single injunction: 'I love these little people, be kind to them.' Following first production on 17 December 1929, he attended several performances of A. A. Milne's stage adaptation, *Toad of Toad Hall*, writing to Curtis Brown after one such, in January 1931, 'I arrived in London stiff as an icicle with cold. I returned glowing with warmth, and with the merry tunes of Toad and his friends dancing through my head.'[16] In November, ahead of a London exhibition, Ernest Shepard wrote 'to ask if you will do me the honour of accepting as a gift, one of the original illustrations that I made for *The Wind in the Willows*'.[17] Kenneth chose the caravan drawing from 'The Open Road'.

Dr Bourdillon had told him enough to make it clear that his own junketings by lane and highway were over.

He died in the early hours of the morning of 6 July 1932, of a cerebral haemorrhage. His death surprised Elspeth, following an unruffled day beside the river and, after supper, a stroll, the two of them, and early bed. The noise that alerted her was Kenneth's book falling from his hand: *The Talisman* by Walter Scott, adored by his grandmother, admired by Cunningham. Elspeth found the book on the floor, Kenneth's bedside lamp still burning, her husband in a coma, past communicating, lost to her, as in truth he had been for much of their marriage.

She arranged the funeral quickly, in Pangbourne's Church of St James the Less, three days after his death; a day of coruscating sunlight that sparkled in dust motes and lit with gold the stands of roses and delphiniums and pale branches of willow gathered that morning from the riverside. Even in so short a time, flowers had arrived from readers across the country, 'with cards attached in a childish scrawl, saying how much they loved him'.[18]

Kenneth was temporarily buried in the churchyard – later, he was transferred to a plot beside Mouse – and quantities of sweet peas heaped the lid of his coffin, their scent incense-heavy, like an opiate, in the heat. 'That nature has her moments of sympathy with man has been noted often enough,' he had written in 1894, in an Olympians story called 'The Blue Room'.[19] So it was the day he was buried. Nature celebrated the final river crossing of this gentle disciple with the full panoply of summer pomp.

Kenneth had excluded Elspeth from *The Wind in the Willows*. At his death she became Penelope at last, weeping and weaving and fixedly attached to his memory. The web that she wove was her own version of his story. The year after he died, she collaborated with Kenneth's first biographer, Patrick Chalmers, to create a hagiography in which past wrongs were righted: this was *Kenneth Grahame: Life, Letters and Unpublished Work*, and she demanded of Chalmers half the book's royalties for her meddling. In 1944, two years before her own death, under the title *First Whisper of 'The Wind in the Willows'*, she published misleading, saccharine 'memories' of her life as wife and mother, Mouse's genius, a version of Kenneth's working practice and the novel's sunshine inspiration. Delusions had made Elspeth's marriage bearable and many of her delusions stemmed from love. But Kenneth had written the stories of his life already, for he lived, as he wrote, in his imagination, this eternal boy acclaimed by Q as 'at once a child and a king'. In imagination, if not in life, he was frequently alone.

Acknowledgements

An award from The Society of Authors assisted the writing of this book. To the Society, and particularly members of the distinguished awards panel, I express my grateful thanks.

I am grateful to the staff of the Bodleian Library, University of Oxford, and also to the Duchess of Argyll.

As always I express heartfelt thanks to my terrific agent, Georgina Capel, and my wonderfully supportive family: my parents, my son Aeneas and my peerless, inspirational, adored wife, Gráinne.

'When the girl returned, some hours later, she carried a tray, with a cup of fragrant tea steaming on it; and a plate piled up with very hot buttered toast, cut thick, very brown on both sides, with the butter running through the holes in it in great golden drops, like honey from the honeycomb. The smell of that buttered toast simply talked to Toad, and with no uncertain voice; talked of warm kitchens, of breakfasts on bright frosty mornings, of cosy parlour firesides on winter evenings [...] of the purring of contented cats, and the twitter of sleeping canaries' (Kenneth Grahame, *The Wind in the Willows*).

MATTHEW DENNISON

Montgomeryshire
Feast of Thomas the Apostle, 2018

Bibliography

The largest collection of archive material relating to the life of Kenneth Grahame is housed in the Bodleian Library, University of Oxford. Patrick Chalmers's 1933 biography, written with Elspeth Grahame's active involvement, quotes a number of primary sources that have since been lost.

Published sources

Batchelor, John, *The Edwardian Novelists* (Duckworth, London, 1982).

Blount, Margaret, *Animal Land: Creatures of Children's Fiction* (Hutchinson, London, 1974).

Carpenter, Humphrey, *Secret Gardens: A Study of the Golden Age of Children's Literature* (Unwin paperback, London, 1985).

Chalmers, Patrick R., *Kenneth Grahame: Life, Letters and Unpublished Work* (Methuen, London, 1933).

Gooderson, David, intro, *My Dearest Mouse: 'The Wind in the Willows' Letters* (Pavilion, London, 1988).

Graham, Eleanor, *Kenneth Grahame* (The Bodley Head, London, 1963).

Grahame, Elspeth, *First Whisper of 'The Wind in the Willows'* (Methuen, London, 1944).

Grahame, Georgina, *In a Tuscan Garden* (The Bodley Head, London, 1903).

Green, Peter, *Kenneth Grahame 1859–1932: A Study of his Life, Work and Times* (John Murray, London, 1959).

— *Beyond the Wild Wood: The World of Kenneth Grahame, Author of The Wind in the Willows* (Webb & Bower, Exeter, 1982).

Greg, Thomas Tylston, *Through a Glass Lightly* (Dent & Company, London, 1897).

Haining, Peter, intro., *Paths to the River Bank: The Origin of The Wind in the Willows* (Blandford Press reprint, London, 1988).

Hunt, Peter, *The Making of The Wind in the Willows* (Bodleian Library, Oxford, 2018).

Hunter, Nicola, & Burkey, Neil, *St Edward's: 150 Years* (Third Millennium Information, 2013).

Kuznets, Lois R., *Kenneth Grahame* (Twayne Publishers, Boston, 1987).

Kynaston, David, *Till Time's Last Sand: A History of the Bank of England 1694–2013* (Bloomsbury, London, 2017).

Lewis, Naomi, intro, *The Penguin Kenneth Grahame* (Penguin, London, 1983).

Marsh, Jan, *Back to the Land: The Pastoral Impulse in Victorian England from 1880 to 1914* (Quartet, London, 1982).

O'Neill, Morna, and Hatt, Michael, ed., *The Edwardian Sense: Art, Design, and Performance in Britain, 1910–1910* (The Yale Center for British Art, Yale University Press, New Haven & London, 2010).

Paterson, Michael, *Inside Dickens' London* (David & Charles, London, 2011).

Preston, Kerrison, ed., *Letters from Graham Robertson* (Hamish Hamilton, London, 1953).

Prince, Alison, *Kenneth Grahame: An Innocent in the Wild Wood* (Allison & Busby, London, 1984).

Rowse, A. L., *Quiller Couch: A Portrait of 'Q'* (Methuen, London, 1988).

Sloan, John, *John Davidson, First of the Moderns* (Clarendon Press, Oxford, 1995).

Thwaite, Ann, *A. A. Milne: His Life* (Faber & Faber, London, 1990).

PERIODICALS

Avery, Gillian, 'The Quest for Fairyland', *The Quarterly Journal of the Library of Congress*, vol 38, no 4 (Fall 1981).

Braybrooke, Neville, 'Kenneth Grahame 1859–1932', *Elementary English*, vol 36, no 1 (January 1959).

Craik, Roger, 'Green and Dying in Chains: Dylan Thomas's "Fern Hill" and Kenneth Grahame's *The Golden Age*', *Twentieth Century Literature*, vol 44, no 3 (Autumn, 1998).

Hintz, Carrie, 'Reviewed Work(s): *The Fantastic Sublime: Romanticism and Transcendence in Nineteenth-Century Children's Fantasy Literature* by David Sandner', *Utopian Studies*, vol 8, no 2 (1997).

Kimball, Miles A., 'Aestheticism, Pan, and Edwardian Children's Literature', *CEA Critic*, vol 65, no 1 (Fall 2002).

Leah, Gordon, 'The Gift of Forgetfulness', *The Furrow*, vol 56, no 5 (May, 2005).

Lerer, Seth, 'Style and the Mole: Domestic Aesthetics in "The Wind in the Willows"', *The Journal of Aesthetic Education*, vol 43, no 2 (Summer 2009).

Mandler, Peter, 'Against "Englishness": English Culture and the Limits to Rural Nostalgia, 1850–1940', *Transactions of the Royal Historical Society*, vol 7 (1997).

Meyers, Jeffrey, 'The Wind in the Willows: A New Source for Animal Farm', *Salmagundi*, no 162/3 (Spring–Summer 2009).

Moore, John David, 'Pottering about in the Garden: Kenneth Grahame's Version of Pastoral in "The Wind in the Willows"', *The Journal of Midwest Modern Language Association*, vol 23, no 1 (Spring 1990).

Perrot, Jean, 'Pan and Puer Aeternus: Aestheticism and the Spirit of the Age', *Poetics Today*, vol 13, no 1 (Spring 1992).

Schlobin, Roger C., 'Danger and Compulsion in the "Wind in the Willows", or Toad and Hyde Together At Last', *Journal of the Fantastic in the Arts*, vol 8, no 1 (29) (1997).

Smith, Kathryn A., 'Kenneth Grahame and the Singing Willows', *Elementary English*, vol 45, no 8 (December 1968).

Steig, Michael, 'At the Back of "The Wind in the Willows": An Experiment in Biographical and Autobiographical Interpretation', *Victorian Studies*, vol 24, no 3 (Spring 1981).

Stein, Ruth M., 'The Changing Styles in Dragons – from Fáfnir to Smaug', *Elementary English*, vol 45, no 2 (February 1968).

Stevenson, Laura C., 'Literary Ladies in the Golden Age of Children's Books', *The Sewanee Review*, vol 119, no 3 (Summer 2011).

Stridsberg, Albert Borden, 'On Illustrating Kenneth Graham', *The Yale University Library Gazette*, vol 24, no 1 (July 1949).

Sullivan III, C. W., '"Chops,... Cheese, New Bread, Great Swills of Beer": Food and Home in Kenneth Grahame's "The Wind in the Willows"', *Journal of the Fantastic in the Arts*, vol 15, no 2 (58) (Spring 2005).

Notes

CHAPTER I

1 Grahame, Kenneth, 'Marginalia' (*Pagan Papers*, The Bodley Head, reprint 1898), pp 76–7.

2 Grahame, Kenneth, 'A Departure' (*Dream Days*, reprinted in *The Penguin Kenneth Grahame*, intro Naomi Lewis, Penguin, London, 1983), p 173.

3 Grahame, Kenneth, 'Marginalia', p 78.

4 Grahame, Kenneth, 'A Saga of the Seas' (*Dream Days*, reprinted in *The Penguin Kenneth Grahame*, intro Naomi Lewis, Penguin, London, 1983), p 136.

5 Grahame, Kenneth, 'Saturnia Regna', *New Review*, vol 14, no 82, March 1896.

6 Ibid.

7 Grahame, Kenneth, review of Evelyn Sharp's *All the Way to Fairyland*, *Academy*, 18 December 1897.

8 Grahame, Kenneth, introduction to Sanger, George, *Seventy Years a Showman* (J. M. Dent, London, 1926), see Bodleian Library, MS Eng. misc. d. 525.

9 Grahame, Kenneth, *The Wind in the Willows* (Methuen, London, 1908, reprinted The Reprint Society, London, 1954), p 212.

10 Grahame, Kenneth, 'Prologue: The Olympians' (*The Golden Age*, reprinted in *The Penguin Kenneth Grahame*, intro Naomi Lewis, Penguin, London, 1983), p 4.

11 Grahame, Kenneth, introduction to *A Hundred Fables of Aesop*,
    in Haining, Peter, intro, *Paths to the River Bank: The Origin
    of The Wind in the Willows* (Blandford Press reprint, London,
    1988), p 61.

12 Grahame, Kenneth, 'Saturnia Regna', *New Review*, vol 14,
    no 82, March 1896.

13 Grahame, Kenneth, 'Orion' (*Pagan Papers*, The Bodley Head,
    reprint 1898), p 187; 'The Magic Ring' (*Dream Days*, reprinted
    in *The Penguin Kenneth Grahame*, intro Naomi Lewis, Penguin,
    London, 1983), p 118.

14 Chalmers, Patrick R., *Kenneth Grahame: Life, Letters and
    Unpublished Work* (Methuen, London, 1933), p 77.

15 Ibid., p 76.

16 Grahame, Kenneth, 'A Saga of the Seas' (*Dream Days*,
    reprinted in *The Penguin Kenneth Grahame*, intro Naomi
    Lewis, Penguin, London, 1983), p 140.

17 Ibid.

18 See Carpenter, Humphrey, *Secret Gardens: A Study of the
    Golden Age of Children's Literature* (Unwin paperback, London,
    1985), p 117.

19 Grahame, Kenneth, 'Prologue: The Olympians' (*The Golden
    Age*, reprinted in *The Penguin Kenneth Grahame*, intro Naomi
    Lewis, Penguin, London, 1983), p 4.

20 Chalmers, Patrick R., op cit., p 2.

21 Grahame, Kenneth, 'The Reluctant Dragon' (*Dream Days*,
    The Bodley Head, London, 1898, reprint Armada, London,
    1972), p 39.

22 Chalmers, Patrick R., op cit., p 5.

23 Ibid., p 4.

24 Grahame, Kenneth, 'The Romance of the Rail' (*Pagan Papers*,
    The Bodley Head, reprint 1898), p 21.

25 Grahame, Kenneth, *The Wind in the Willows* (Methuen, London, 1908, reprinted The Reprint Society, London, 1954), p 169; on this connection, see Green, Peter, *Kenneth Grahame 1859–1932: A Study of his Life, Work and Times* (John Murray, London, 1959), p 11.

26 Prince, Alison, *Kenneth Grahame: An Innocent in the Wild Wood* (Allison & Busby, London, 1984), p 7.

27 Grahame, Kenneth, *The Wind in the Willows* (Methuen, London, 1908, reprinted The Reprint Society, London, 1954), p 4.

28 Prince, Alison, op cit., p 7.

29 Grahame, Kenneth, 'The Mountain Stream' (poem), *Hull Weekly News*, 15 April 1905 – see Bodleian Library, MS Eng. misc. d. 525 (146).

30 Grahame, Kenneth, 'Loafing' (*Pagan Papers*, The Bodley Head, reprint 1898), p 45.

Chapter 2

1 Grahame, Kenneth, introduction to Sanger, George, *Seventy Years a Showman* (J. M. Dent, London, 1926), see Bodleian Library, MS Eng. misc. d. 525.

2 Grahame, Kenneth, 'A Departure' (*Dream Days*, reprinted in *The Penguin Kenneth Grahame*, intro Naomi Lewis, Penguin, London, 1983), p 169.

3 Quoted in Chalmers, Patrick R., op cit., p 174.

4 Grahame, Kenneth, 'The Romance of the Rail' (*Pagan Papers*, The Bodley Head, reprint 1898), p 26.

5 Kenneth Graham to Kitty Cheatham, undated letter, Bodleian Library, MS Eng. misc. d. 527 (16); 'The Romance of the Rail' (*Pagan Papers*, The Bodley Head, reprint 1898), p 28.

6 Grahame, Kenneth, 'A Departure' (*Dream Days*, reprinted in *The Penguin Kenneth Grahame*, intro Naomi Lewis, Penguin, London, 1983), p 175.

7   Hamilton, Clayton, 'A Personal Appreciation of Kenneth Grahame', see Bodleian Library, MS Eng. misc. c. 380 (162).

8   Green, Peter, op. cit., p 137.

9   Graham, Eleanor, *Kenneth Grahame* (The Bodley Head, London, 1963), p 12.

10 See Chalmers, Patrick R., op cit., p 8; Green, Peter, op cit., p 17.

11 Green, Peter, op cit., p 23 and p 27.

12 See Graham, Eleanor, op cit., p 14.

13 Quoted in Chalmers, Patrick R., op cit., p 271.

14 Grahame, Kenneth, 'The Magic Ring' (*Dream Days*, reprinted in *The Penguin Kenneth Grahame*, intro Naomi Lewis, Penguin, London, 1983), p 120; Chalmers, Patrick R., op cit., p 70, p 132, p 25.

15 Green, Peter, op cit., p 20.

16 Grahame, Kenneth, 'Sawdust and Sin' (*The Golden Age*, reprinted in *The Penguin Kenneth Grahame*, intro Naomi Lewis, Penguin, London, 1983), p 25.

17 Quoted in Chalmers, Patrick R., op cit., p 265.

18 Quoted in Graham, Eleanor, op cit., p 14.

19 Grahame, Kenneth, 'A Departure' (*Dream Days*, reprinted in *The Penguin Kenneth Grahame*, intro Naomi Lewis, Penguin, London, 1983), p 171.

20 Bodleian Library, MS Eng. misc. d. 525.

21 Grahame, Kenneth, 'The Reluctant Dragon' (*Dream Days*, reprinted in *The Penguin Kenneth Grahame*, intro Naomi Lewis, Penguin, London, 1983), p 146.

22 See Green, Peter, op cit., pp 17–18.

23 Stevenson, Robert Louis, *Virginibus Puerisque* (1881, reprint Penguin 1946), p 69.

24 Grahame, Kenneth, 'The Romance of the Rail' (*Pagan Papers*, The Bodley Head, reprint 1898), p 27.

25 Grahame, Kenneth, 'The Magic Ring' (*Dream Days*, reprinted in *The Penguin Kenneth Grahame*, intro Naomi Lewis, Penguin, London, 1983), p 118.

26 Grahame, Kenneth, 'Prologue: The Olympians' (*The Golden Age*, reprinted in *The Penguin Kenneth Grahame*, intro Naomi Lewis, Penguin, London, 1983), pp 3–5.

27 Grahame, Kenneth, 'Justifiable Homicide' (*Pagan Papers*, The Bodley Head, reprint 1898), p 147.

28 Grahame, Kenneth, 'A Falling Out' (*The Golden Age*, reprinted in *The Penguin Kenneth Grahame*, intro Naomi Lewis, Penguin, London, 1983), p 80.

CHAPTER 3

1 Grahame, Kenneth, 'Lusisti Satis' (*The Golden Age*, reprinted in *The Penguin Kenneth Grahame*, intro Naomi Lewis, Penguin, London, 1983), p 80.

2 Prince, Alison, op cit., p 29.

3 Grahame, Kenneth, 'The Twenty-First of October' (*The Golden Age*, reprinted in *The Penguin Kenneth Grahame*, intro Naomi Lewis, Penguin, London, 1983), p 93.

4 Grahame, Kenneth, 'The Reluctant Dragon' (*Dream Days*, The Bodley Head, London, 1898, reprint Armada, London, 1972), p 7.

5 Grahame, Kenneth, 'Cheap Knowledge' (*Pagan Papers*, The Bodley Head, reprint 1898), p 59.

6 Grahame, Kenneth, 'The Spell of Oxford', July 1932, see Bodleian Library, MS Eng. misc. d. 525 (63–77).

7 Grahame, Kenneth, 'Lusisti Satis' (*The Golden Age*, reprinted in *The Penguin Kenneth Grahame*, intro Naomi Lewis, Penguin, London, 1983), p 86.

8 Grahame, Kenneth, 'The Fairy Wicket' (*Pagan Papers*, The Bodley Head, reprint 1898), p 158.

9 Ibid.

10 Grahame, Kenneth, 'The Spell of Oxford', July 1932,
    see Bodleian Library, MS Eng. misc. d. 525 (63–77).

11 Grahame, Kenneth, 'Alarums and Excursions' (*The Golden
    Age*, reprinted in *The Penguin Kenneth Grahame*, intro Naomi
    Lewis, Penguin, London, 1983), p 18.

12 Grahame, Kenneth, 'The Fairy Wicket' (*Pagan Papers*,
    The Bodley Head, reprint 1898), p 158.

13 Grahame, Kenneth, 'The Spell of Oxford', July 1932,
    see Bodleian Library, MS Eng. misc. d. 525 (63–77).

14 Hunter, Nicola, & Burkey, Neil, *St Edward's: 150 Years* (Third
    Millennium Information, 2013), p 13.

15 Green, Peter, op cit., p 94.

16 Grahame, Kenneth, 'Orion' (*Pagan Papers*, The Bodley Head,
    reprint 1898), p 188.

17 Grahame, Kenneth, 'Lusisti Satis' (*The Golden Age*, reprinted
    in *The Penguin Kenneth Grahame*, intro Naomi Lewis,
    Penguin, London, 1983), p 88.

18 Ibid., p 89.

19 Hunter & Burkey, op cit., p 13; Grahame, Kenneth, 'Marginalia'
    (*Pagan Papers*, The Bodley Head, reprint 1898), p 78; Bodleian
    Library, MS Eng. misc. d. 525 (94).

20 Prince, Alison, op cit., p 33.

21 Chalmers, Patrick R., op cit., p 131.

22 Grahame, Kenneth, 'The Twenty-First of October' (*The
    Golden Age*, reprinted in *The Penguin Kenneth Grahame*, intro
    Naomi Lewis, Penguin, London, 1983), p 93; ibid., 'Lusisti
    Satis', p 90.

23 Grahame, Kenneth, 'The Spell of Oxford', July 1932,
    see Bodleian Library, MS Eng. misc. d. 525 (63–77).

24 Ibid.

25 Chalmers, Patrick R., op cit., p 23.

26 See Bodleian Library, MS Eng. misc. d. 525.

27 Grahame, Kenneth, *The Wind in the Willows* (Methuen, London, 1908, reprinted The Reprint Society, London, 1954), p 211.

28 Grahame, Kenneth, 'Cheap Knowledge' (*Pagan Papers*, The Bodley Head, reprint 1898), p 56.

29 Chalmers, Patrick R., op cit., pp 26–7; Grahame, Kenneth, 'The Eternal Whither' (*Pagan Papers*, The Bodley Head, reprint 1898), p 91.

30 Grahame, Kenneth, 'The Spell of Oxford', July 1932, see Bodleian Library, MS Eng. misc. d. 525 (63–77).

31 Green, Peter, *Beyond the Wild Wood: The World of Kenneth Grahame* (Webb & Bower, Exeter, 1982), p 38.

32 Grahame, Kenneth, 'Marginalia' (*Pagan Papers*, The Bodley Head, reprint 1898), p 79.

33 Green, Peter, op cit., *Kenneth Grahame*, p 37.

34 Grahame, Kenneth, 'Its Walls were as of Jasper' (*Dream Days*, reprinted in *The Penguin Kenneth Grahame*, intro Naomi Lewis, Penguin, London, 1983), p 135; ibid., 'Dies Irae', p 105.

35 Kenneth Grahame to Methuen & Co, 24 December 1931, see Bodleian Library, MS Eng. misc. d. 527 (194).

36 Grahame, Kenneth, 'Its Walls were as of Jasper' (*Dream Days*, reprinted in *The Penguin Kenneth Grahame*, intro Naomi Lewis, Penguin, London, 1983), p 135.

37 Chalmers, Patrick R., op cit., pp 30–31.

CHAPTER 4

1 Green, Peter, op cit., *Kenneth Grahame*, p 356, n 8.

2 Grahame, Kenneth, 'The Eternal Whither' (*Pagan Papers*, The Bodley Head, reprint 1898), p 90.

3 Chalmers, Patrick R., op cit., p 28.

4 Grahame, Kenneth, 'The White Poppy' (*Pagan Papers*, The Bodley Head, reprint 1898), p 125.

5   Grahame, Kenneth, 'The Romance of the Road' (*Pagan Papers*, The Bodley Head, reprint 1898), p 16.

6   Grahame, Kenneth, 'Justifiable Homicide' (*Pagan Papers*, The Bodley Head, reprint 1898), p 151–2.

7   Grahame, Kenneth, 'Dies Irae' (*Dream Days*, reprinted in *The Penguin Kenneth Grahame*, intro Naomi Lewis, Penguin, London, 1983), p 103.

8   Grahame, Kenneth, 'Saturnia Regna', *New Review*, vol 14, no 82, March 1896.

9   Ibid.

10 Grahame, Kenneth, *The Wind in the Willows* (Methuen, London, 1908, reprinted The Reprint Society, London, 1954), p 229.

11 Grahame, Kenneth, 'The Finding of the Princess' (*The Golden Age*, reprinted in *The Penguin Kenneth Grahame*, intro Naomi Lewis, Penguin, London, 1983), p 23.

12 Chalmers, Patrick R., op cit., p 264.

13 See Kuznets, Lois R., *Kenneth Grahame* (Twayne Publishers, Boston, 1987), p 27.

14 Grahame, Kenneth, 'The Inner Ear', in Haining, Peter, intro, op cit., p 89.

15 Grahame, Kenneth, 'Cheap Knowledge' (*Pagan Papers*, The Bodley Head, reprint 1898), p 57–8.

16 Quoted in Chalmers, Patrick R., op cit., pp 129–36.

17 Ibid., p 52.

18 Green, Peter, op cit., *Kenneth Grahame*, p 61.

19 Ibid., p 201.

20 Grahame, Kenneth, 'Non Libri Sed Liberi' (*Pagan Papers*, The Bodley Head, reprint 1898), p 32.

21 Grahame, Kenneth, 'Sawdust and Sin' (*The Golden Age*, reprinted in *The Penguin Kenneth Grahame*, intro Naomi Lewis, Penguin, London, 1983), p 25.

22 Grahame, Kenneth, *The Wind in the Willows* (Methuen, London, 1908, reprinted The Reprint Society, London, 1954), p 233.

23 Grahame, Kenneth, 'The Secret Drawer' (*The Golden Age*, reprinted in *The Penguin Kenneth Grahame*, intro Naomi Lewis, Penguin, London, 1983), p 66.

CHAPTER 5

1 Grahame, Kenneth, 'The Eternal Whither' (*Pagan Papers*, The Bodley Head, reprint 1898), p 86.

2 Paterson, Michael, *Inside Dickens' London* (David & Charles, London, 2011), p 98.

3 Grahame, Kenneth, 'The Eternal Whither' (*Pagan Papers*, The Bodley Head, reprint 1898), p 85; ibid., 'A Bohemian in Exile', pp 134–6; 'Long Odds', *The Yellow Book*, July 1895; 'Orion', pp 188–9.

4 Grahame, Kenneth, 'The Headswoman', *The Yellow Book*, October 1894.

5 Kenneth Grahame to Curtis Brown, 11 November 1928, Bodleian Library, MS Eng. misc. d. 526 (136).

6 Grahame, Kenneth, 'The Rural Pan' (*Pagan Papers*, The Bodley Head, reprint 1898), p 65.

7 Quoted in Chalmers, Patrick R., op cit., p 272.

8 Grahame, Kenneth, 'The Inner Ear', in Haining, Peter, intro, op cit., p 89.

9 Green, Peter, op cit., *Beyond the Wild Wood*, p 61.

10 Prince, Alison, op cit., p 59.

11 Chalmers, Patrick R., op cit., p 47.

12 Grahame, Kenneth, 'Its Walls were as of Jasper' (*Dream Days*, reprinted in *The Penguin Kenneth Grahame*, intro Naomi Lewis, Penguin, London, 1983), p 129.

13 Grahame, Kenneth, 'The Romance of the Road' (*Pagan Papers*, The Bodley Head, reprint 1898), p 16.

14 Green, Peter, op cit., *Beyond the Wild Wood*, p 64, p 44.

15 Grahame, Kenneth, *The Wind in the Willows* (Methuen, London, 1908, reprinted The Reprint Society, London, 1954), p 80.

16 See Lerer, Seth, 'Style and the Mole: Domestic Aesthetics in "The Wind in the Willows"', *The Journal of Aesthetic Education*, vol 43, no 2 (Summer 2009), p 59.

17 Grahame, Kenneth, 'Dies Irae' (*Dream Days*, reprinted in *The Penguin Kenneth Grahame*, intro Naomi Lewis, Penguin, London, 1983), p 105.

18 See Bodleian Library, MS Eng. misc. c. 380 (45).

19 Grahame, Kenneth, 'Cheap Knowledge' (*Pagan Papers*, The Bodley Head, reprint 1898), p 55.

20 Green, Peter, op cit., *Kenneth Grahame*, p 87.

21 Grahame, Kenneth, *The Wind in the Willows* (Methuen, London, 1908, reprinted The Reprint Society, London, 1954), p 82.

22 Green, Peter, op cit., *Kenneth Grahame*, p 88.

23 Grahame, Kenneth, 'The Reluctant Dragon' (*Dream Days*, The Bodley Head, London, 1898, reprint Armada, London, 1972), p 7.

24 Grahame, Kenneth, 'Loafing' (*Pagan Papers*, The Bodley Head, reprint 1898), p 49; Smith, Kathryn A., 'Kenneth Grahame and the Singing Willows', *Elementary English*, vol 45, no 8 (December 1968), p 1031.

25 Grahame, Kenneth, introduction to Sanger, George, *Seventy Years a Showman* (J. M. Dent, London, 1926), see Bodleian Library, MS Eng. misc. d. 525.

26 Grahame, Kenneth, 'Loafing' (*Pagan Papers*, The Bodley Head, reprint 1898), p 52.

27 Grahame, Kenneth, 'A Bohemian in Exile' (*Pagan Papers*, The Bodley Head, reprint 1898), pp 137–8.

28 Green, Peter, op cit., *Kenneth Grahame*, p 93.

NOTES

29 Ibid., p 94.

30 Grahame, Kenneth, 'Of Smoking' (*Pagan Papers*, The Bodley Head, reprint 1898), p 109, p 103.

31 Green, Peter, op cit., *Kenneth Grahame*, p 86.

32 Green, Peter, op cit., *Beyond the Wild Wood*, p 66.

33 Chalmers, Patrick R., op cit., p 37.

34 Green, Peter, op cit., *Kenneth Grahame*, p 88; Chalmers, Patrick R., op cit., p 110.

35 Grahame, Kenneth, 'The Secret Drawer' (*The Golden Age*, reprinted in *The Penguin Kenneth Grahame*, intro Naomi Lewis, Penguin, London, 1983), p 67.

36 Green, Peter, op cit., *Beyond the Wild Wood*, p 76.

37 Grahame, Kenneth, 'The Secret Drawer' (*The Golden Age*, reprinted in *The Penguin Kenneth Grahame*, intro Naomi Lewis, Penguin, London, 1983), pp 66–7.

38 Ibid., p 67.

39 Forster, E. M., *The Longest Journey* (Edward Arnold, London, 1907, reprint Penguin, London, 1983), p 147.

40 Grahame, Kenneth, 'A Harvesting' (*The Golden Age*, reprinted in *The Penguin Kenneth Grahame*, intro Naomi Lewis, Penguin, London, 1983), p 41.

41 Grahame, Kenneth, *The Wind in the Willows* (Methuen, London, 1908, reprinted The Reprint Society, London, 1954), p 127.

42 Ibid.

43 Grahame, Kenneth, 'Saturnia Regna', *New Review*, vol 14, no 82, March 1896.

CHAPTER 6

1 Quoted in Chalmers, Patrick R., op cit., p 249.

2 Grahame, Kenneth, 'The Roman Road' (*The Golden Age*, reprinted in *The Penguin Kenneth Grahame*, intro Naomi Lewis, Penguin, London, 1983), p 58.

3   Chalmers, Patrick R., op cit., p 234.

4   Grahame, Kenneth, 'The Twenty-First of October' (*Dream Days*, reprinted in *The Penguin Kenneth Grahame*, intro Naomi Lewis, Penguin, London, 1983), p 96; Chalmers, Patrick R., op cit., p 250.

5   Grahame, Kenneth, *The Wind in the Willows* (Methuen, London, 1908, reprinted The Reprint Society, London, 1954), p 214.

6   Prince, Alison, op cit., p 83.

7   Grahame, Kenneth, *The Wind in the Willows* (Methuen, London, 1908, reprinted The Reprint Society, London, 1954), p 226–7.

8   Grahame, Georgina, *In a Tuscan Garden* (The Bodley Head, London, 1903).

9   Grahame, Kenneth, 'By a Northern Furrow', *St James's Gazette*, 21 December 1888.

10 Green, Peter, op cit., *Kenneth Grahame*, p 98.

11 Chalmers, Patrick R., op cit., p 238, p 249.

12 Grahame, Kenneth, 'The Reluctant Dragon' (*Dream Days*, The Bodley Head, London, 1898, reprint Armada, London, 1972), p 30.

13 Grahame, Kenneth, *The Wind in the Willows* (Methuen, London, 1908, reprinted The Reprint Society, London, 1954), p 218.

14 Quoted in Chalmers, Patrick R., op cit., p 38.

15 Green, Peter, op cit., *Kenneth Grahame*, p 99.

16 Grahame, Kenneth, 'A Bohemian in Exile' (*Pagan Papers*, The Bodley Head, reprint 1898), p 143.

17 Chalmers, Patrick R., op cit., p 46.

18 Grahame, Kenneth, 'A Saga of the Seas' (*Dream Days*, reprinted in *The Penguin Kenneth Grahame*, intro Naomi Lewis, Penguin, London, 1983), p 143.

19 Green, Peter, op cit., *Beyond the Wild Wood*, p 82.

20 Stevenson, Robert Louis, op cit., p 152.

21 Green, Peter, op cit., *Kenneth Grahame*, p 114; Stevenson, Robert Louis, op cit., dedication.

22 Green, Peter, op cit., *Kenneth Grahame*, p 143.

23 Green, Peter, op cit., *Beyond the Wild Wood*, p 84.

24 See Bodleian Library, MS Eng. misc. c. 380 (162).

25 Grahame, Elspeth, *First Whisper of 'The Wind in the Willows'* (Methuen, London, 1944), p 27.

Chapter 7

1 Grahame, Kenneth, 'Of Smoking' (*Pagan Papers*, The Bodley Head, reprint 1898), p 105.

2 Green, Peter, op cit., *Beyond the Wild Wood*, p 87.

3 See Bodleian Library, MS Eng. misc. c. 380; Chalmers, Patrick R., op cit., p 215.

4 Smith, Kathryn A., op cit., p 1029.

5 Green, Peter, op cit., *Kenneth Grahame*, p 9.

6 Quoted in Hunt, Peter, *The Making of The Wind in the Willows* (Bodleian Library, Oxford, 2018), p 35.

7 Grahame, Kenneth, *The Wind in the Willows* (Methuen, London, 1908, reprinted The Reprint Society, London, 1954), p 126.

8 W. D. Livesay, 12 August 1908, Bodleian Library, MS Eng. misc. d. 531 (83).

9 Prince, Alison, op cit., p 147; Chalmers, Patrick R., op cit., p 80.

10 Grahame, Kenneth, 'The Romance of the Road' (*Pagan Papers*, The Bodley Head, reprint 1898), pp 17–18.

11 Chalmers, Patrick R., op cit., p 78.

12 Stevenson, Robert Louis, op cit., p 136.

13 Prince, Alison, op cit., p 101.

14 Green, Peter, op cit., *Kenneth Grahame*, p 134.

15 Prince, Alison, op cit., p 102.

16 Grahame, Kenneth, 'The Rural Pan' (*Pagan Papers*, The Bodley Head, reprint 1898), p 69.

17 See Mandler, Peter, 'Against "Englishness": English Culture and the Limits to Rural Nostalgia, 1850–1940', *Transactions of the Royal Historical Society*, vol 7 (1997), p 107.

18 Grahame, Kenneth, 'Deus Terminus' (*Pagan Papers*, The Bodley Head, reprint 1898), pp 96–8.

19 Chalmers, Patrick R., op cit., p 66.

20 Sloan, John, *John Davidson, First of the Moderns* (Clarendon Press, Oxford, 1995), pp 101–2.

21 Grahame, Kenneth, 'The Reluctant Dragon' (*Dream Days*, The Bodley Head, London, 1898, reprint Armada, London, 1972), pp 45–6.

22 See Bodleian Library, MS Eng. misc. c. 380 (124) (Evelyn Sharp Nevinson).

23 Prince, Alison, op cit., p 361 n 15.

24 Green, Peter, op cit., *Kenneth Grahame*, p 152.

25 Chalmers, Patrick R., op cit., p 55.

26 Green, Peter, op cit., *Kenneth Grahame*, p 152.

27 Grahame, Kenneth, 'The Reluctant Dragon' (*Dream Days*, The Bodley Head, London, 1898, reprint Armada, London, 1972), p 39.

28 Ibid., pp 18–19.

29 Ibid., p 44.

CHAPTER 8

1 Grahame, Kenneth, 'The Magic Ring' (*Dream Days*, reprinted in *The Penguin Kenneth Grahame*, intro Naomi Lewis, Penguin, London, 1983), p 124.

2   Grahame, Kenneth, 'The Fellow That Walks Alone',
    in Haining, Peter, intro, op cit., p 68.

3   Grahame, Kenneth, *The Wind in the Willows* (Methuen,
    London, 1908, reprinted The Reprint Society, London, 1954),
    p 11.

4   Ibid., p 10; Chalmers, Patrick R., op cit., p 158.

5   Greg, T. T., *Through a Glass Lightly* (Dent & Company,
    London, 1897); Grahame, Kenneth, 'The Fellow That Walks
    Alone', in Haining, Peter, intro, op cit., p 68.

6   Grahame, Elspeth, op cit., p 30.

7   Green, Peter, op cit., *Kenneth Grahame*, p 21.

8   Grahame, Kenneth, 'Its Walls were as of Jasper' (*Dream Days*,
    reprinted in *The Penguin Kenneth Grahame*, intro Naomi
    Lewis, Penguin, London, 1983), p 128.

9   Grahame, Kenneth, 'A Saga of the Seas' (*Dream Days*,
    reprinted in *The Penguin Kenneth Grahame*, intro Naomi
    Lewis, Penguin, London, 1983), p 143.

10 Prince, Alison, op cit., p 114.

11 Ibid., p 112.

12 Grahame, Kenneth, 'The Fairy Wicket' (*Pagan Papers*,
    The Bodley Head, reprint 1898), p 161.

13 Prince, Alison, op cit., p 135.

14 Grahame, Kenneth, 'Its Walls were as of Jasper' (*Dream Days*,
    reprinted in *The Penguin Kenneth Grahame*, intro Naomi
    Lewis, Penguin, London, 1983), p 134.

15 Grahame, Kenneth, 'Mutabile Semper' (*Dream Days*, reprinted
    in *The Penguin Kenneth Grahame*, intro Naomi Lewis, Penguin,
    London, 1983), p 117.

16 Grahame, Kenneth, 'Its Walls were as of Jasper' (*Dream Days*,
    reprinted in *The Penguin Kenneth Grahame*, intro Naomi
    Lewis, Penguin, London, 1983), p 135.

17 See Bodleian Library, MS Eng. misc. c. 380.

18 Prince, Alison, op cit., p 16; Green, Peter, op cit., *Kenneth Grahame*, p 217.

19 'The Reluctant Dragon', also included in the sequence and written at the same time, is essentially a stand-alone piece.

20 Grahame, Kenneth, 'A Departure' (*Dream Days*, reprinted in *The Penguin Kenneth Grahame*, intro Naomi Lewis, Penguin, London, 1983), pp 170–71.

21 'Love's Reveille', poem, *National Observer*, 27 February 1892.

CHAPTER 9

1   Elspeth Thomson to Kenneth Grahame, undated 1899, Bodleian Library, MS Eng. misc. e. 480 (1).

2   Ibid.

3   Kenneth Grahame to Austin Purves, 3 November 1908, quoted in Chalmers, Patrick R., op cit., p 219.

4   Elspeth Thomson to Kenneth Grahame, undated 1899, Bodleian Library, MS Eng. misc. e. 480 (1).

5   See Green, Peter, op cit., *Kenneth Grahame*, p 207.

6   Kenneth Grahame to Elspeth Thomson, undated ('Monday morning') 1899, Bodleian Library, MS Eng. misc. e. 480 (5).

7   Kenneth Grahame to Elspeth Thomson, undated 1899, Bodleian Library, MS Eng. misc. e. 480 (9).

8   Kenneth Grahame to Elspeth Thomson, undated 1899, Bodleian Library, MS Eng. misc. e. 480 (23).

9   Kenneth Grahame to Elspeth Thomson, undated 1899, Bodleian Library, MS Eng. misc. e. 480 (26).

10 Kenneth Grahame to Elspeth Thomson, undated 1899, Bodleian Library, MS Eng. misc. e. 480 (24).

11 Kenneth Grahame to Elspeth Thomson, undated 1899, Bodleian Library, MS Eng. misc. e. 480 (27).

12 Kenneth Grahame to Elspeth Thomson, undated 1899, Bodleian Library, MS Eng. misc. e. 480 (24).

13   Kenneth Grahame to Elspeth Thomson, undated 1899,
     Bodleian Library, MS Eng. misc. e. 480 (30).

14   Kenneth Grahame to Elspeth Thomson, undated 1899,
     Bodleian Library, MS Eng. misc. e. 480 (32).

15   Ibid.

16   Kenneth Grahame to Elspeth Thomson, undated 1899,
     Bodleian Library, MS Eng. misc. e. 480 (35).

17   Green, Peter, op cit., *Kenneth Grahame*, p 227.

18   Ibid.

19   Kenneth Grahame to Elspeth Thomson, undated 1899,
     Bodleian Library, MS Eng. misc. e. 480 (37).

20   Kenneth Grahame to Elspeth Thomson, undated 1899,
     Bodleian Library, MS Eng. misc. e. 480 (41).

21   Kenneth Grahame to Elspeth Thomson, undated 1899,
     Bodleian Library, MS Eng. misc. e. 480 (47).

22   Elspeth Thomson, 'Accepted', poem, Bodleian Library,
     MS Eng. misc. c. 381 (105).

23   Kenneth Grahame to Elspeth Thomson, undated 1899,
     Bodleian Library, MS Eng. misc. e. 480 (47).

24   Kenneth Grahame to Elspeth Thomson, undated 1899,
     Bodleian Library, MS Eng. misc. e. 480 (69).

25   Green, Peter, op cit., *Kenneth Grahame*, p 215.

26   Kenneth Grahame to Elspeth Thomson, undated 1899,
     Bodleian Library, MS Eng. misc. e. 480 (93, 90).

27   Green, Peter, op cit., *Kenneth Grahame*, p 216.

28   Kenneth Grahame to Elspeth Thomson, undated 1899,
     Bodleian Library, MS Eng. misc. e. 480 (47).

29   Grahame, Kenneth, *The Wind in the Willows* (Methuen,
     London, 1908, reprinted The Reprint Society, London, 1954),
     pp 227–8.

30   Kenneth Grahame to Elspeth Thomson, undated 1899,
     Bodleian Library, MS Eng. misc. e. 480 (61).

31 Prince, Alison, op cit., p 165.

32 Chalmers, Patrick R., op cit., p 237.

33 Kenneth Grahame to Elspeth Thomson, undated 1899, Bodleian Library, MS Eng. misc. e. 480 (57).

34 Kenneth Grahame to Austin Purves, 8 July 1912, quoted in Chalmers, Patrick R., op cit., pp 239–40; Green, Peter, op cit., *Kenneth Grahame*, p 227; Kenneth Grahame to Austin Purves, 7 February 1911, quoted in Chalmers, Patrick R., op cit., p 234.

35 Kenneth Grahame to Austin Purves, 20 September 1911, quoted in Chalmers, Patrick R., op cit., p 237.

36 Green, Peter, op cit., *Kenneth Grahame*, p 227.

CHAPTER 10

1   See Tomalin, Claire, *Thomas Hardy: The Time-torn Man* (Penguin paperback, London, 2007), p 431 n 30.

2   Green, Peter, op cit., *Kenneth Grahame*, p 217.

3   Ibid., p 216.

4   Grahame, Kenneth, 'Sawdust and Sin' (*The Golden Age*, reprinted in *The Penguin Kenneth Grahame*, intro Naomi Lewis, Penguin, London, 1983), p 27.

5   Bodleian Library, MS Eng. misc. d. 525.

6   Chalmers, Patrick R., op cit., p 75; Grahame, Kenneth, 'The Magic Ring' (*Dream Days*, reprinted in *The Penguin Kenneth Grahame*, intro Naomi Lewis, Penguin, London, 1983), p 126.

7   Kenneth Grahame to Elspeth Thomson, undated 1899, Bodleian Library, MS Eng. misc. e. 480 (47).

8   Green, Peter, op cit., *Kenneth Grahame*, p 226.

9   Quoted in Prince, Alison, op cit., p 141.

10 Bodleian Library, MS Eng. misc. c. 380 (162).

11 Grahame, Kenneth, 'The Roman Road' (*The Golden Age*, reprinted in *The Penguin Kenneth Grahame*, intro Naomi Lewis, Penguin, London, 1983), p 58.

12 Green, Peter, op cit., *Kenneth Grahame*, pp 225–6.

13 Elspeth Thomson, 'Ah Happy Eyes', poem, Bodleian Library, MS Eng. misc. c. 381 (108).

14 Elspeth Thomson, 'It would provoke a saint', poem, Bodleian Library, MS Eng. misc. c. 381 (107).

15 Elspeth Thomson, 'I'm quite sure if you only knew', poem, Bodleian Library, MS Eng. misc. c. 381 (129).

16 Elspeth Thomson, 'Rejected', poem, Bodleian Library, MS Eng. misc. c. 381 (110).

17 Elspeth Thomson, 'Give me a kiss that will last for ever', poem, Bodleian Library, MS Eng. misc. c. 381 (130).

18 Hunt, Peter, op cit., p 40.

19 Grahame, Kenneth, *The Wind in the Willows* (Methuen, London, 1908, reprinted The Reprint Society, London, 1954), p 313.

20 Prince, Alison, op cit., p 196.

21 Green, Peter, op cit., *Beyond the Wild Wood*, p 178.

22 Kenneth Grahame to Austin Purves, 24 August 1910, quoted in Chalmers, Patrick R., op cit., p 228.

23 Grahame, Elspeth, op cit., p 17.

24 Green, Peter, op cit., *Kenneth Grahame*, p 326.

25 Chalmers, Patrick R., op cit., p 149.

CHAPTER 11

1 Graham, Eleanor, op cit., p 38.

2 Kenneth Grahame to Elspeth Grahame, undated, see Bodleian Library, MS Eng. misc. e. 481; Prince, Alison, op cit., p 189.

3 Kenneth Grahame to Elspeth Grahame, undated, see Bodleian Library, MS Eng. misc. e. 481 (24).

4 Kenneth Grahame to Elspeth Grahame, undated, see Bodleian Library, MS Eng. misc. e. 481 (91).

5 Grahame, Elspeth, op cit., p 46.

6 Ibid., p 10.

7   Prince, Alison, op cit., p 206.

8   Ibid.

9   Quoted in Chalmers, Patrick R., op cit., p 98.

10 Green, Peter, op cit., *Kenneth Grahame*, p 226; Grahame, Elspeth, op cit., p 38.

11 Green, Peter, op cit., *Kenneth Grahame*, p 115.

12 Kenneth Grahame to Elspeth Grahame, undated, see Bodleian Library, MS Eng. misc. e. 481 (12).

13 Kenneth Grahame to Elspeth Grahame, undated, see Bodleian Library, MS Eng. misc. e. 481 (17).

14 Prince, Alison, op cit., p 209.

15 Ibid., p 199.

16 Green, Peter, op cit., *Kenneth Grahame*, p 236.

17 Grahame, Elspeth, op cit., p 3.

18 Green, Peter, op cit., *Beyond the Wild Wood*, p 178.

19 Grahame, Elspeth, op cit., p 7.

CHAPTER 12

1   Grahame, Elspeth, op cit., p 49, p 88.

2   Hunt, Peter, op cit., p 54.

3   Ibid., p 51.

4   Smedley, Constance, *An April Princess* (Cassell & Co, London, 1903).

5   See Gooderson, David, intro, *My Dearest Mouse: 'The Wind in the Willows' Letters* (Pavilion, London, 1988), p 11.

6   Green, Peter, op cit., *Kenneth Grahame*, p 269.

7   Gooderson, David, op cit., p 11.

8   Grahame, Elspeth, op cit., p 30.

9   Green, Peter, op cit., *Beyond the Wild Wood*, p 166.

10 Graham Robertson to Kenneth Grahame, undated (1908), see Bodleian Library, MS Eng. misc. d. 529 (17).

11 Graham Robertson to Kenneth Grahame, undated (1908), see Bodleian Library, MS Eng. misc. d. 529 (13).

12 Hunt, Peter, op cit., p 86.

13 Ibid., p 47.

14 Ibid.

15 *Times Literary Supplement*, 22 October 1908.

16 Kenneth Grahame to Austin Purves, 17 December 1908, quoted in Chalmers, Patrick R., op cit., p 221.

17 Kenneth Grahame to Miss Francois, 31 January 1909, see Bodleian Library, MS Eng. misc. d. 527 (54).

18 Ibid.

19 Hunt, Peter, op cit., p 88.

20 Kenneth Grahame to Austin Purves, 3 November 1908, quoted in Chalmers, Patrick R., op cit., p 220.

21 Green, Peter, op cit., *Beyond the Wild Wood*, p 179.

22 Grahame, Kenneth, *The Wind in the Willows* (Methuen, London, 1908, reprinted The Reprint Society, London, 1954), p 36.

23 Ibid., p 274.

24 Kenneth Grahame to Miss Gullett, 20 May 1913, see Bodleian Library, MS Eng. misc. d. 527 (83).

25 Green, Peter, op cit., *Kenneth Grahame*, p 274.

CHAPTER 13

1 Green, Peter, op cit., *Beyond the Wild Wood*, p 186.

2 Alistair Grahame, letter to his parents, 23 July 1911, see Bodleian Library, MS Eng. misc. d. 527; Grahame, Kenneth, 'Loafing' (*Pagan Papers*, The Bodley Head, reprint 1898), p 49; Chalmers, Patrick R., op cit., p 154.

3 Chalmers, Patrick R., op cit., p 205; Grahame, Kenneth, 'The Reluctant Dragon' (*Dream Days*, The Bodley Head, London, 1898, reprint Armada, London, 1972), p 15.

4 Grahame, Kenneth, 'Loafing' (*Pagan Papers*, The Bodley Head, reprint 1898), p 47.

5 Chalmers, Patrick R., op cit., p 223.

6 Grahame, Kenneth, 'The Fellow That Walks Alone', in Haining, Peter, intro, op cit., p 69.

7 Grahame, Kenneth, *The Wind in the Willows* (Methuen, London, 1908, reprinted The Reprint Society, London, 1954).

8 Grahame, Kenneth, 'The Fellow That Walks Alone', in Haining, Peter, intro, op cit., p 69.

9 Quoted in Green, Peter, op cit., *Kenneth Grahame*, p 277.

10 Kenneth Grahame to Austin Purves, 27 July 1909, quoted in Chalmers, Patrick R., op cit., p 222.

11 Kenneth Grahame to Curtis Brown, 22 January 1920, see Bodleian Library, MS Eng. misc. d. 526 (130).

12 Kenneth Grahame to Austin Purves, 30 September 1910, quoted in Chalmers, Patrick R., op cit., p 230.

13 Alistair Grahame, letter to his parents, undated 1910, see Bodleian Library, MS Eng. misc. e. 482 (91).

14 Kenneth Grahame to Austin Purves, 20 May 1910, quoted in Chalmers, Patrick R., op cit., p 225.

15 Kenneth Grahame to Kitty Cheatham, undated, see Bodleian Library, MS Eng. misc. d. 527 (16).

16 Kenneth Grahame to Austin Purves, 20 May 1910, quoted in Chalmers, Patrick R., op cit., p 225.

17 Grahame, Elspeth, op cit., pp 17–18.

18 Green, Peter, op cit., *Kenneth Grahame*, p 292.

19 Green, Peter, op cit., *Beyond the Wild Wood*, p 185; see Bodleian Library, MS Eng. misc. d. 530 (182).

20 Green, Peter, op cit., *Beyond the Wild Wood*, p 205.

21 Grahame, Kenneth, 'The Fellow That Walks Alone', in Haining, Peter, intro, op cit., p 67.

22 Grahame, Kenneth, *The Wind in the Willows* (Methuen, London, 1908, reprinted The Reprint Society, London, 1954), p 232.

23 Bodleian Library, MS Eng. misc. d. 527 (106).

24 Kenneth Grahame to Austin Purves, 2 August 1910, quoted in Chalmers, Patrick R., op cit., pp 226–7.

25 Bodleian Library, MS Eng. misc. c. 380 (162).

26 Kenneth Grahame to Curtis Brown, 22 January 1920, see Bodleian Library, MS Eng. misc. d. 526 (130).

27 See Graham Robertson's reply, Bodleian Library, MS Eng. misc. d. 529.

28 Quoted in Prince, Alison, op cit., p 274.

29 Kenneth Grahame to Austin Purves, 27 July 1909, quoted in Chalmers, Patrick R., op cit., p 222.

30 Prince, Alison, op cit., p 351.

31 Green, Peter, op cit., *Kenneth Grahame*, p 304.

32 Ibid., p 305.

CHAPTER 14

1 Chalmers, Patrick R., op cit., p 235.

2 Prince, Alison, op cit., p 261.

3 Alistair Grahame to his parents, 11 June 1911, see Bodleian Library, MS Eng. misc. d. 527.

4 Kenneth Grahame to Austin Purves, 16 August 1911, quoted in Chalmers, Patrick R., op cit., p 236.

5 Ibid.

6 Kenneth Grahame to Austin Purves, 12 January 1911, quoted in Chalmers, Patrick R., op cit., p 232.

7 Kenneth Grahame to Austin Purves, 15 May 1911, quoted in Chalmers, Patrick R., op cit., p 234.

8 Quoted in Prince, Alison, op cit., p 283.

9   Alistair Grahame to his parents, 15 October 1911, see Bodleian Library, MS Eng. misc. d. 527.

10 Alistair Grahame to his parents, 10 December 1911, see Bodleian Library, MS Eng. misc. d. 527.

11 Alistair Grahame to Kenneth Grahame, 'Xmas 1912', see Bodleian Library, MS Eng. misc. d. 527.

12 Prince, Alison, op cit., p 305.

13 Quoted in Prince, Alison, op cit., p 284.

14 Alistair Grahame to Elspeth Grahame, 5 July 1914, see Bodleian Library, MS Eng. misc. d. 527.

15 A. R. Waller to Kenneth Grahame, 19 March 1913, see Bodleian Library, MS Eng. misc. d. 526.

16 John Lane to Kenneth Grahame, undated, see Bodleian Library, MS Eng. misc. d. 526 (56).

17 Prince, Alison, op cit., p 352.

18 Kenneth Grahame to A. R. Waller, undated, see Bodleian Library, MS Eng. misc. d. 526 (32).

19 Green, Peter, op cit., *Kenneth Grahame*, p 319.

20 Prince, Alison, op cit., p 286.

21 Graham Robertson to Kenneth Grahame, undated, see Bodleian Library, MS Eng. misc. d. 529 (25).

22 Ibid.

23 Green, Peter, op cit., *Kenneth Grahame*, p 316.

24 Ibid.

25 Ibid.

26 Ibid., p 318.

27 Kenneth Grahame to Austin Purves, 18 February 1915, quoted in Chalmers, Patrick R., op cit., p 247.

28 Grahame, Kenneth, 'The Fellow That Walks Alone', in Haining, Peter, intro, op cit., p 67.

29 Grahame, Kenneth, speech in aid of French Red Cross Fund, 1918, see Bodleian Library, MS Eng. misc. d. 525 (87).

CHAPTER 15

1   Kenneth Grahame to Curtis Brown, 29 April 1926,
    see Bodleian Library, MS Eng. misc. d. 526 (134).

2   Kenneth Grahame to A. J. A. Symons, 16 July 1926,
    see Bodleian Library, MS Eng. misc. d. 527 (62).

3   See Bodleian Library, MS Eng. misc. c. 381 (120).

4   Chalmers, Patrick R., op cit., p 256.

5   Quoted in Chalmers, Patrick R., op cit., p 262.

6   See Bodleian Library, MS Eng. misc. c. 525 (97); Prince,
    Alison, op cit., p 350.

7   See Bodleian Library, MS Eng. misc. c. 525 (97).

8   Arthur Quiller-Couch to Kenneth Grahame, 17 August 1925,
    see Bodleian Library, MS Eng. misc. c. 381 (156).

9   Prince, Alison, op cit., p 179.

10 Guy Pocock to Kenneth Grahame, 11 September 1925,
    see Bodleian Library, MS Eng. misc. d. 526 (151).

11 Grahame, Kenneth, introduction to Sanger, George, *Seventy
    Years a Showman* (J. M. Dent, London, 1926), see Bodleian
    Library, MS Eng. misc. d. 525.

12 Prince, Alison, op cit., p 329.

13 Grahame, Elspeth, op cit., p 27.

14 Chalmers, Patrick R., op cit., p 317.

15 Quoted in Green, Peter, op cit., *Kenneth Grahame*, p 346.

16 Kenneth Grahame to Curtis Brown, 8 January 1931,
    see Bodleian Library, MS Eng. misc. d. 526.

17 Ernest Shepard to Kenneth Grahame, November 1931,
    see Bodleian Library, MS Eng. misc. d. 530 (201).

18 Green, Peter, op cit., *Kenneth Grahame*, p 349.

19 Grahame Kenneth, 'The Blue Room' (*The Golden Age*,
    reprinted in *The Penguin Kenneth Grahame*, intro Naomi
    Lewis, Penguin, London, 1983), p 73.

Index

INDEX

Payn, James 101–2
Pinturicchio 60, 96
Pitlochry, Scotland 61, 62, 97
Pocock, Guy 239
Potter, Beatrix: *The Tale of Peter Rabbit* 189, 194
Presbyterianism 24
Punch 84, 135, 197
Purves, Austin 190, 194, 195–6, 207–8, 212, 213, 223, 226–7, 238
Purves, Betsy 194
Pyrenees 173

Quarry Wood, Berkshire 23–4, 27, 205
Quiller-Couch, Arthur 'Q' 159–60, 161, 173, 181, 183, 200, 206, 218, 222, 223, 225, 238, 241, 243
Quiller-Couch, Bevill 218, 238

Raeburn, Henry 103
'Reluctant Dragon, The' vii, 11, 38, 80–1, 123, 127–8, 172
Richardson, Mary 91, 92
Robert the Bruce 10
Robertson, Graham 180–1, 192–3, 194, 206, 212, 223, 224, 225, 226
Roberts, Tom 93
Rodd, Sir Rennell 235
'Romance of the Road, The' 55, 114, 115

'Roman Road, The' 123, 169
Rome, Italy 97, 234–5, 236
Roosevelt, Theodore 190, 195, 198
Rural Pan, The' 59, 72, 103, 119
Ruskin, John 60, 77; *The Stones of Venice* 77

'Saga of the Seas, A' 7–8, 102, 144
Sala, George Augustus: *Twice Round the Clock; or the Hours of the Day and Night in London* 70
Sanger, George 21, 239
Sargent, John Singer 180–1
'Sawdust and Sin' 121, 166
Scotland *see individual area or place name*
Scots Observer 103, 111, 118
Scott, Walter 12, 21, 242
Scribner's Magazine 126
'Secret Drawer, The' 86
Shakespeare, William 38, 223, 241
Sharp, Evelyn 108, 124, 125–6, 138, 144
Shaw, George Bernard 95
Shelley, Percy Bysshe 235, 241; *The Cenci* 95–6, 123, 135
Shelley Society 95
Shepard, E. H. 241
Simpson, Dr James 9–10
Sitwell, Osbert 237–8